A Coaching Business In A Book

A Coaching Business In A Book

Sarah Short
The Coaching Revolution

Published by The Coaching Revolution 2020
TheCoachingRevolution.com

ISBN: 978-1-9163701-1-1

Typeset by Fuzzy Flamingo
www.fuzzyflamingo.co.uk

A catalogue for this book is available from the British Library.

For the missing Revolutionary. In loving memory of Paul Hancock (Hank), without whom The Coaching Revolution would never have existed.

Hank, I miss our conversations, your wit and your pragmatic approach to life. Rest in peace my lovely friend.

Contents

To be a coach, one must have clients. To have a successful coaching business, those clients must be ones who pay.

Sarah Short, The Coaching Revolution

Introduction

In September 2017, Paul Snell, Paul Hancock and I were all working as coaches and making our living doing so. We were also spitting mad.

We were sick, sick, sick of the snake-oil pedlars that exist in the world of business development training for coaches. We thought that there was a place for sensible, pragmatic business development advice for coaches and we decided that we would start The Coaching Revolution to help some UK-based coaches earn some money from their coaching.

Little did we know what was going to happen. We were blown away by those who came to seek our help. At the time of writing, we are under three years old and we are supporting coaches all over the world – quite literally from Bogota to Brisbane – to grow successful businesses.

Our business development process isn't new; companies in every sector use it. However, what we've done is hone it for coaches. We've also found ourselves working with consultants, and they too have found success using our honed method.

In this book you will learn everything you need to grow a coaching business. You will learn how to create a business that is financially, as well as emotionally fulfilling. If you read it and then cherry pick the bits that you take from it, I can't assure you of the outcome. If, on the other hand, you implement everything I tell you, in the way I describe, you will have success.

It's that simple.

Becoming Visible

I know you.

You're a coach. You're absolutely passionate about coaching, because you've seen it transform lives (not least of which is your own). I know that you love to help people and that coaching is the *perfect* way for you to help.

You want to coach people to help them to achieve a life of more than mediocrity; you want people to live full, rewarding, challenging lives. Lives which are both meaningful and joyful.

And yet, you can't find clients who want to pay you.

Not Another Coaching Book

Let me be clear, this is not just another coaching book. It's not a book about coaching technique at all, because I don't believe the world needs that book. To be honest, I'm not the most experienced coach in the world and I think it would be disingenuous of me to pretend that I can add something meaningful or unique to coaching technique.
What this book is, is a book about how to get clients if you're a coach. This is an area in which I have not only lots of experience, but also the insight of the experiences of

hundreds and hundreds of other coaches with whom I have either worked or talked to. This is a book about marketing yourself and selling your services and it's for coaches. It's written specifically with you in mind.

Why You Need Clients

It stands to reason that if you can't find clients, you can't coach them. If you can't coach them, then those clients, those people that are waiting for you to help them transform their lives will remain stuck where they are. What a terrible waste of opportunity that would be. How awful for those people to not live their best lives because you can't find them.

The good news is that your clients are waiting for you. You don't believe me, do you? Let me tell you why what I say is true.

When they start their coaching businesses, most coaches build websites that are simply online CVs. Some of them are beautiful, I grant you, but they are *all about the coach*. Coaches can spend a fortune on these websites, and you know what? They rarely, if ever, generate clients. The reason for this is that the website becomes another, anonymous website, lost among the three **trillion** URLs (yes, you read that number correctly) that are out there.
Your clients are **not** looking for you. They're waiting for you, but they're not looking for you. Mostly because they have no idea about coaching. They also have absolutely no idea that you are there, waiting to support them to change their lives.

How Do You Find Those Who Are Waiting?

The million-dollar question is how do you find these clients?

Well, the way that your clients find you, is by you finding them. That sounds double-Dutch, doesn't it, but let me explain. You need to stop being a generalist, a coach for everyone, and become a specialist, a coach for one kind of client. If you do, you'll find that your clients have a problem that you can help them with. They know they have this problem, but they don't yet know that coaching is the solution. Actually, they don't even care that coaching is the solution, they just want the problem that they have to be gone.

As their coach, your job is to be where they are, and to support them to see what life could look like for them without this particular problem; the specific problem that you can solve for them with coaching. For example, maybe you're a career coach. Well, there are thousands of career coaches, what makes you so special? The best bit about the answer to that question is that you get to decide what makes you special.
Maybe you want to work with young professionals who are moving from their first job to their next one. Or perhaps you want to work with those who have had a successful career but want to move into a completely different industry or profession. Or possibly you want to work with those who know that they are heading for retirement, but before they retire, they know that they have one really good job left in them.

As a coach, you get to choose who you want to work with. All of them could use some coaching from you, but each one needs very different help. They also need to hear very different things in order to understand *why* they could use some coaching.

Clients don't care about the coaching process; clients care about a solution to their problems. Your clients are waiting with a problem that only you can help them to solve.

Coaches on the other hand, **do** care about the coaching process and can wax lyrical about it for hours. If they wax lyrical about it to any of the potential clients that I've just described, they will watch, disappointed, as that person glazes over, stops listening and ceases to be a potential client.

There is a reason why 82% of coaches fail to create successful businesses and it's because they don't know how to become visible to their clients.

Social Media

We are all aware of the many social media platforms that are available to us and the incredible reach that it gives to those who use it wisely. We also see other coaches posting on LinkedIn, Instagram, Facebook and the rest and they look so successful, don't they? They talk about their clients and how much they're enjoying their lives and their coaching businesses.

I see coaches posting on social media all the time (I admit it, I'm a coach-stalker!) and I can spot a coach who isn't making a living from coaching, based entirely on what they write.

Those who post about mental barriers, and reaching goals,

about limiting beliefs and resilience; they're not doing well. The ones who use social media 'hopefully' aren't doing well either (think memes that say *dream big, and you will achieve,* or *if you can dream it, you can achieve it,* and worst of all – in my humble opinion – *what one thing can I help you with today?*).

Those who speak directly to one particular kind of client, they're on the mark. That laser-focus is absolutely necessary to get results; and make no mistake, the results I'm talking about are paying clients.

Marketing well is a rare art amongst coaches. By the time you reach the end of this book and providing you've taken the actions I give you, you will know exactly what to say, who you're saying it to, and on which platform you need to say it, to make sure that the kind of clients you want to work with hear you. Your marketing will be generating that most wonderful of things, the holy grail of coach-marketing; inbound enquiries.

Your social media content will actually result in people hopping into your inbox and asking if they can talk to you. They'll *want* to talk to you! Not only that, they'll want to talk to you about coaching! How fabulous will that be?

Why You Need To Read This Book

The purpose of this book is to teach you, step by step, how to create a financially viable coaching business. A fair question to ask would be *what do you mean by financially viable?* The answer to this question is once again, that you get to choose.

Can you generate your first £10k using the method we teach? Absolutely you can. Can you generate your first £100k? Absolutely you can. The difference between your first £10k and your first £100k is the length of time it takes to get there. They are two points on the road to which this book is the map. Follow the map to the letter and you will generate paying clients.

The important thing to remember is that you need to be known for **one** thing. You need to promote **one** kind of coaching, to **one** client. Before you faint, remember, this isn't forever, it's for *now*. You don't have to only ever coach one kind of person, but – and here's the thing – *you have to start somewhere*.

You and Your Coaching

Somehow, we found coaching. All of us did. If you're reading this book, you've found coaching.

I believe that coaching is a superpower. It transforms lives and I think that makes it a superpower. Anyone or anything that can achieve what coaching can, really needs to be given the title of 'superpower'.

If coaching was a drug that was available on prescription, everyone would want it. Imagine a drug so powerful that it can help you see exactly what you want from life and support you in reaching that destination. That would be one best-selling drug, right? We who have discovered coaching know that what I just described is the effect of good coaching. And we want in!

What those who become coaches have in common, is that we are usually 'people people'. This kind of person has a natural inclination towards helping others and when they discover coaching, what they see is that there's a whole profession available to them, one that's all about helping people be the best they can be. It's not surprising that many teachers, medical professionals and those from other 'helping' sectors become coaches. Coaching supports individuals to become the very best version of themselves, so what people-person wouldn't be attracted to it? Coaching is a forward-looking, positive and uplifting experience for both coach and client. I think it's why those who have spent years working in the medical profession (particularly in therapy) love coaching. That forward-focus can be more uplifting than the backward-looking, painful reflection can be for both therapist and patient. I believe that coaching is perfect work.

The myriad of different journeys to becoming a coach have remarkably similar beginnings. I've spoken to literally thousands of coaches and their stories usually start out one of two ways. Some of us will have been coached at work, as part of our performance enhancement. Others may have a friend who took a coaching course and who asked us if we'd mind helping them out by being coached.

There are other routes too, of course. I once spoke to a person who watched a Tony Robbins video on a Saturday night, and spoke to me on the Monday to say that they wanted to be *just like Tony!* Imagine their disappointment when I suggested that first, they may need to get a coaching qualification and some experience under their belt.

Anyway, whichever way we got here, once we found coaching, we were never the same again.

The Coaching Revolution

The Coaching Revolution works with people who have a coaching qualification (or are either taking one or prepared to take one) to teach them how to build a coaching business that can support them financially. We know that what we do works, and we only want to work with people who understand what coaching is and they need to have, or be prepared to acquire, good coaching skills.

There are many coaching qualifications available from institutions all over the world. The courses they offer may have different titles, and they may go about delivering training in different ways, but what they have in common is that they enable an ordinary human being – like you and me – to develop our superpower to a level that is worthy of a professional qualification.

Client-Focused

Coaching courses are all about how the client should be the sole focus of any coaching conversation. Everything we're taught revolves around the client and the moment. We look at coaching agreements (contracts), both formal and informal. We look at ethics, and in that study, we talk about how our ethics impacts the client and other stakeholders in the coaching relationship.

On our coaching courses, we talk about fees (although we rarely talk about pricing) and we talk about how we might interact with different stakeholders, in different kinds of coaching relationships. For example, if an organisation is paying for the coaching, they may want some kind of report from the coach. Clearly, if the client knows that what they say will be reported back to their boss, they may be reluctant to speak their truth in coaching sessions. So, we talk about how to craft a coaching agreement to allow both confidentiality and reporting at the same time.

Coaches are taught active listening skills, which are practised, honed and polished throughout the course. We're taught the importance of being judgement-free. Coaches learn about creating a space to allow the client to explore their thoughts and feelings without fear of judgement or criticism. The coach learns to be curious. We learn how to ask questions that make the client think.

Good coaching questions can stop a client in their tracks and create lightbulb moments so bright that the whole room is illuminated in the moment. The client can move from confusion and feeling stuck, to clarity, purpose and determination in an instant.

Honestly, good coaching really is a superpower.

The purpose of this book is not to raise one form of coaching qualification above others. I'm not going to say that one coach is better than another based on the flavour of their coaching qualification. The purpose of this book is to talk about what happens to coaches after they finish their qualification. Specifically, the purpose of this book is to explain what happens to coaches in the majority of cases (that they fail to find coaching clients) and why that happens. It is also to show you what to do, so that you are not one of the majority of coaches who fails to thrive.

Assumptions Make An Ass...

We are taught to coach with an assumption from all parties (training provider and student) that we'll walk out of the classroom and into a coaching space to start work. All this talk of stakeholders, and interested parties, and who will pay for what, and how important it is to get clarity on everything in our coaching agreements, means that there is a high expectation on the part of the coach that their coaching clients will be waiting outside the classroom door on their final day of study. *When we finish our qualifications, we leave, clutching our new, shiny certificate and our hearts are full of joy. We've succeeded! We are now coaches! The missions of new coaches are remarkably similar, in that they simply want to improve the lives of others through coaching.*

Nothing could be further from the truth.

Failure Rates Amongst Coaches

There is an ICF global statistic that says that 82% of coaching businesses fail in their first two years. Let's think about that for a minute. What that means is that for every 10 of your coaching course cohort, fewer than two of them will actually go on to coach for a living.

Most coaching is done on a freelance (or self-employed) basis. What that means is the coach needs to become self-employed and then get out there and find clients who want to pay them for their coaching.

I can hear you protesting loudly that there are employed coaching roles available, and to an extent you're right. However, employed coaches often have a corporate agenda to which they need to adhere. There are other types of roles that have the title coach, but actually have nothing whatsoever to do with coaching. The UK's Department for

Work and Pensions, for example, employs people as 'work coaches' but actually, they are the clerks who process unemployment claims and issue sanctions for breaches of the rules. They don't coach in the way you and I mean when we talk about coaching.

The are other people who refer to themselves as coaches, but who aren't in the way we mean, are several sorts of business coaches. They offer advice on business processes and may be offered out by Chambers of Commerce to start ups, that sort of thing. I know a few of these advisors and some are actually qualified coaches. The rest are simply people, some really good and experienced, others less so (and in some cases, a **lot** less so!).

Of course, there are employed coaching roles for the kind of coaching we are referring to, where the coach doesn't have a corporate agenda. Those roles are few and far between and the competition for them is fierce. Coaches with literally thousands of logged hours apply for these roles and those of us who are reasonably newly qualified, don't really stand a chance of getting them.

Let's go back to that 82%. If we can for the purposes of this conversation, accept that coaches are often self-employed, then we need to take note of that number. Let's break that 82% to a meaningful smaller figure. Those small figures break my heart: Four out of five coaches will fail. Four out of five big-hearted, other-people-centred individuals with whom we took our coaching courses will fail.

The question of course, has to be why do so many coaches qualify and then fail to thrive in the coaching industry?

The answer to this question is remarkably simple. **Coaches fail because they have no business development skills.** It is possible to be a fantastic coach, the very best coach ever in fact and still fail, because coaching, and *the business of coaching* are two very separate and different skillsets.

Our Websites

Once we've come to terms with our new status of coach, the work has to begin. We are forward-focused and happy that everyone will want to work with us. We sit down and create our coaching brand. We spend our money on websites, on branding and on photos.

On our websites, we describe:

- our coaching packages,
- how we work with people
- what our prices are
- how we deliver coaching
- our coaching qualification(s)

We set the website up and we put any testimonials that we have (even if they're from other coaching course buddies – they're still testimonials, right?). We set up our social media platforms and make sure that our branding is consistent across them all. Some coaches even set up limited companies and register themselves for VAT. Finally, once all the preparation is done, we're ready to go. Watch out world, here we come!

This is the point at which many coaches suddenly flounder. What are they supposed to do next? There is a kind of fog around what has to happen next. How does one go from being ready to earn, to actually earning?

Certainly, we can post on social media, and there is no shortage of coaches who post what I have already referred to as 'hopeful' posts. What I mean are things like *what one thing can I help you with today?* or *what's stopping you from living the life of your dreams?* Sometimes these posts get engagement, but I've yet to meet the coach who gained paying clients from this type of post.

However, social media aside, what is a coach supposed to **do** to get clients?

When we reflect back on our coaching course from a position of knowledge and experience, we realise that although we were very client-centred in everything we learned, how those clients arrived in the room was not discussed, it was simply *assumed* that they were there.

Occasionally, a coach-training provider will touch upon business development. They may talk about delivering free sessions; those initial sessions designed to get the client to talk about goals and what they can do to achieve them. The idea is that the potential client will be so thrilled with the conversation, that they will be desperate to become your client. These sessions tend to be called discovery sessions, or strategy sessions. In one case I heard a coach calling this a chemistry session. There are various terms for these free initial coaching sessions, but the outcome is the same; you may pick up the odd client this way, but the number of free sessions you need to deliver in order to create a viable coaching business is **huge.** As a business development tool, particularly if it's your only tool, it's poor

Case Study

Let me give you an example of why I believe that discovery sessions are a poor way of growing a coaching business.

I recently became involved in an online conversation between a group of coaches who are now qualified and on a quest to find paying clients. One of them, a newly qualified coach, was proudly telling the others about her endeavours to find paying clients and the fantastic success that she'd had. She said that she had posted like mad for a whole month all over a variety of social media, offering free coaching sessions to anyone who'd like one. She had 28 people say that they'd like a session (to be delivered virtually). Of the 28, 20 actually showed up – the other 8 didn't cancel, they just didn't show up. From that 20, she secured 3 paying clients. She also said that the other 17 were 'delighted' with their free session.

If we look at that in a little more detail, we can see the following:

- One month spent generating and distributing content across social media, let's say 2 hours a day; 40 hours (she can have the weekends off – I'm good like that!).
- Time spent booking 28 people into a diary (or maybe there was an online scheduler that she used – not sure), shall we say an hour?
- 28 x 1 hours allocated to delivering 1:1 sessions.
- 20+ hours actually delivering, or sitting, waiting to deliver. (Let's say 22 in total?)
- 3 x paying clients and 17 non-paying, but delighted.

What we can see here is that this coach spent 40 hours creating/posting content, an hour scheduling, 22 hours delivering (or waiting to deliver). That's 67 hours – and out of it, she got 3 clients. If those clients are each spending a terrific sum, then great, but otherwise, that's a lot of time spent gaining 3 clients.

The coach in question charges £95 per session and each of the three clients signed up for a monthly session for 3 months. That's 9 sessions in total, so £285pm or a total of £855 over 3 months. That's £12.76 per hour. If you're coaching for pin-money (that's pocket money if you're not British) this is fine. If you have all the time in the world and you both enjoy the process, and don't need to live on your income, that's also fine. If, like most of us, you can't possibly live on £285pm, it is an unsustainable process.

Those 17 delighted ones? They mean nothing. Brutal, but true. It is highly unlikely that they will either come back for coaching or refer people to her, even though they said they would. I'm not being mean, I'm just very experienced.

Why This Business Development Tool Is Poor

What happens to those who employ this marketing technique (and only this technique) is that they deliver free session after free session and eventually, they run out of people to give free sessions to. This can be a bit of a shock because, well, coaching is a superpower, right? We walked out of the classroom and the expectation was that we should have started coaching right away, and yet we now find ourselves in a position where it's getting uncomfortable to persuade people we don't know to let us coach them for free. This is not the way it was supposed to work!

What usually happens next is that the coach thinks *what am I doing wrong? Clearly,* (this thought process goes), *I'm doing something wrong, because if I was doing the right thing, I'd have clients, wouldn't I?*

Then, a massive number of coaches think exactly the same thing. It's actually remarkable how many coaches from different backgrounds and cultures have this same thought. They think this: *I know! I'll take someone through an entire coaching programme for free. That way, they will reach their goals, and I'll have a delighted client from whom I can get a fabulous testimonial. And (*the thought process goes) *this client will be* ***so thrilled*** *that they will recommend me and my amazing coaching to everyone they know! This is a win-win situation.*

I feel like I'm pouring cold water on what has felt like such a fabulous idea for so many coaches all over the world. The problem with this kind of coaching is that it rarely, if ever, works. Let me explain why.

The thing about coaching is that it is about change, and change is difficult. We humans don't like change because it's challenging. The client who is coached for free has no 'skin in the game'. What I mean by this is that this client hasn't spent money on their coaching and so they don't have that underlying feeling of wanting to get their money's worth. This client doesn't have that financial pressure to keep them going when the going gets tough. Skin in the game adds to client 'stickability'. It isn't the be-all and end-all of course, there's a lot more to stickability than a financial commitment. However, those with a financial commitment do have that extra bit of stickability that those without that commitment have, and it does make a difference. There's something about getting something for free that makes us value it a lot less. We just don't take it as seriously, nor do we give it the same level of priority in our lives. Coaching of course, is about the client giving their chosen actions high priority.

What happens with clients who are being coached for free is that when the coaching process gets difficult, they walk away. They rarely say *I'm sorry, this whole change thing is getting uncomfortable, and I want to stop*. No, what happens is that their priorities change. They may start to be unreliable in terms of not having done what they said they would in between sessions. They change and cancel appointments and finally, they stop contacting you and/or responding to your contact.

This leaves the client feeling totally underwhelmed about coaching as a whole and the coach feeling very unhappy. *I don't understand* (the coach thinks) *I can't even give coaching away for free! This is just not what I expected at all.*

Let me describe one possible last step in this process of disillusionment. Having failed spectacularly to get their coaching business off the ground in any meaningful way, the coach may think: *I know what the problem is, I don't know enough so I'm going to take an additional qualification. I'm going to take X, Y or Z qualification. Then I'll have even more to offer to my clients!* For X, Y and Z read any of the myriad of possible coaching, training, facilitating, or profiling courses that are out there. What this coach fails to realise is that it's very difficult to offer more value **to clients that you don't have**!

Balance

If you for a moment, image a pair of old-fashioned weighing scales like the kind that your granny may have had, where you have to make the weight of one side equal the other by adding a little bit at a time until they balance. This is a great analogy for your coaching business.

A coaching qualification is actually only 50% of the skills you need to create a coaching business – the delivery half. Whether you have an entry level qualification, or you've taken every coaching qualification that it's possible to gain, those qualifications all belong on one side of the scale. Here's the rub, no matter how many additional qualifications you take, you are *still* only adding to that one side of the scales. A coach can spend thousands and thousands of dollars and/ or pounds on qualifications, whilst all the time believing that what they're doing is increasing the value that they can offer to their clients (the ones they don't have!) and what they are actually doing, is adding to that one side of the scales. In the end, the scales are so out of balance, that one side – the delivery side of your coaching business – is touching the ground, and the other side is hanging around mid-air.

The Other Side Of The Scale

What then, goes on the other side of the scales? How can a coach find balance in their business? Well, the other 50% of a coaching business is made up of the skills you need to create the opportunities to do the delivery – these are the business development skills that I have mentioned.

Coaches often come from a background of employment, rather than self-employment and this means that they have never had to find their next client. The next client, project or piece of work simply walked through the door and asked for their product or service. Interestingly, even those who have worked in sales and marketing on an employed basis often still find it hard to market and sell themselves as a coach.

The world of self-employment means that you need to find those clients yourself and doing that involves business development.

Business development skills are marketing and sales skills and, just like any other skill, they can be learned. In my experience, coaches don't like these skills. To be honest, they don't even like thinking about them. Specifically, they don't like the idea of selling, or marketing or doing anything at all that may, in their minds, be deemed 'pushy'. This feels incongruous with coaching. Coaches will tell me that they are no good at selling. They tell me that they are an introvert and so therefore automatically lousy at selling, or that they had a job in a shop when they were 16 and they were fired because they couldn't sell (true story!) and they offer that up as the reason their coaching business isn't thriving. Coaches don't want to have to sell, the idea of selling makes them feel grubby. Coaches want clients to simply appear. They'd like nothing better than to be able to magically attract clients.

Enter the Charlatans

Coaches reach the point of desperation when they've delivered countless discovery sessions, they've coached a few people for free and it hasn't gone the way they imagined and finally, they reach the *what am I doing wrong?* point. There was not, at any point during their course, any suggestion that finding coaching clients was going to be in any way tricky, let alone downright impossible. Coaches now start to look for a way of dodging the thing that they fear; having to sell. They start to look for a silver bullet to solve their problem, the one that will result in them being able to simply attract clients.

At this point, coaches resort to looking at two groups of people whom I consider to be charlatans. I don't say this lightly. I say it from a position of experience and knowledge, as well as from countless conversations with coaches.

Charlatans basically come in two guises. The first is the 'proven marketing system' charlatan. These are organisations who seem to offer the perfect solution to struggling coaches. *Join us, and your marketing is sorted! You don't have to worry about getting clients anymore, building a business will be a breeze! Simply learn our marketing presentation and deliver it, and clients will come to you!* Sometimes, there is coaching material associated with this promise. The organisations concerned are basically offering material and a marketing system that, they promise, is a turnkey solution to a coach's marketing problems. These organisations can charge tens of thousands of pounds and in the cases of some, have additional monthly royalty fees. One organisation I know of costs £65k+ to join, with a £2k+ per month royalty, as well as assorted 'additional fees'. Their marketing to coaches is slick, their sales presentations to coaches thinking of joining them, is even slicker. One former member of this particular organisation said that he'd known people lose their homes in order to buy themselves out of the contract they signed to join. The organisation concerned was prepared to allow them to do that. He remarked that any coach that this had happened to, was obliged to sign a non-disclosure agreement (NDA) to prevent them soiling the slick company's international marketing message by actually telling the truth. The truth being, of course, that the system they bought into doesn't work as often as it fails.

Another of these organisations costs much less, but is again based outside the UK. Their message is that they've been doing this successfully, for 30 years. Again, they sell material as well as a 'proven marketing system'. Their system is a presentation, which they encourage their coaches to get out and deliver to absolutely anyone who will listen. This organisation talks at length about the support that their coaches enjoy, and their marketing is littered with testimonials from people like 'John, from London' and 'Terry, from Sydney'. These testimonials talk about how much support they're getting and how excited they are for the future. What you never see are testimonials that talk about success, about how a coach is picking up clients, or about how the 'proven system' is working. The last time I had knowledge of this organisation, 97% of their coaches in the UK had failed to recoup their initial investment. The only ones who were making any income were those selling the system to coaches. Marketing that worked in the 1990s is outdated and is not fit for purpose for the sophisticated consumer of the 21st century.

The Online Guru

The other kind of charlatan is the online guru. I call these people the 'just ONE thing' gurus. They proliferate on Facebook and their message tends to be a version of this: *I was just like you! I was a heart-centred coach, who desperately wanted to help people and yet I just couldn't find paying clients. I was at the end of my tether and then, I discovered this ONE THING, and now I'm a $60k a month coach. I've helped countless others achieve the same thing, give me £$£$£$£ and I can help you too!*

You can probably tell from the way I've paraphrased their words, that I don't hold these people in high regard. Apart from anything else, there isn't ONE THING you need to do to build a coaching business, there are several. In my opinion, these people are vultures who prey on the vulnerable. Make no mistake, by this point in their journey, coaches are vulnerable. I have spoken to many, many coaches who have spent money with this kind of guru and I can tell you that not one of them made their initial investment back.

Let me describe one particularly sad conversation.

A coach – let's call her Angela – told me that she was desperate. She needed some help, and very quickly. She simply had to find paying coaching clients and it was urgent. She needed a guarantee that she'd find clients in the next four weeks.

I explained that this isn't how marketing works, that marketing is a process, not an event and that there is no way that I could ever guarantee that she would finish all the work on her marketing message necessary to get paying clients in four weeks. It is possible of course, but I wasn't prepared to guarantee it. I also needed to understand what the rush was about.

Angela told me that she had contacted a Facebook guru, via a sponsored advertisement and had spoken to the guru in person, on the phone. This guru told Angela that if she joined her organisation, she would be earning 5-figures from month one. The cost of joining the organisation was an eye-watering $30k. Angela asked the guru to promise her that 5-figures was achievable in the first month and this guru promised, in fact, she guaranteed it. Angela explained that she would need that 5-figure sum to pay her usual monthly outgoings, as well as the debt she was about to accrue to join the organisation. Again, the guru guaranteed that what she said was true. Angela, buoyed by the certainty of the guru, put the whole $30k on her credit card.

The guru's system involved Angela abandoning her existing clients (they were small in number, but they did exist), because they were paying only £100 a session, and throwing herself wholeheartedly into 'the system'. By the time the first payment was due on her credit card, Angela was in deficit. Not only had she earned absolutely nothing by following this system, she had lost the few hundred pounds she had been earning from the clients she already had.

I asked her why. Why had she spent the $30k? Why did she believe this – frankly unbelievable – tale of riches? *The guru is a coach, like me,* Angela said. *Coaches are lovely people. Why would she lie to me?* I asked Angela if she'd signed an agreement and her voice became small. Yes, she'd signed an agreement. Did the agreement offer the same guarantee that the guru had offered verbally? Sadly, it didn't. *I thought that her telling me that she guaranteed it meant something,* Angela told me. *I thought it was a verbal contract*. Of course, Angela hadn't recorded the call, why would she? Instead of her 5-figure income, Angela was left with a $30k debt, no clients at all and no immediate plan of how she was going to repay that debt.

My heart broke for this woman. Gullible? Yes. Naive? Of course. Mostly however, Angela was vulnerable. Despicably, the guru smelled that vulnerability and swooped in for the kill.

This conversation made me so angry! How dare this guru take money like this? How dare she prey on coaches who are vulnerable and simply don't know any better? Yes, Angela was far from savvy, but who hasn't made a mistake when they've felt pressure? Let s/he who is without sin, and all that.

I can't definitively say that no one ever does succeed with this kind of guru, but I have never met anyone nor heard of anyone who has and believe me, I've searched for them.

Business Development Training

Let's go back, for a moment, to our qualification providers; in order to maintain balance and to be fair, there are some coach-training providers that do look at business development. They may mention that you need a *niche* or very occasionally, they might mention the idea of having an *ideal client*. However, even if a training provider has an entire module dedicated to business development, that's not enough. Remember 50% – a full half – of the skills a coach needs are business development skills.

May I interrupt myself here to say that to be fair to training providers, their job is to teach us how to coach, not teach us how to sell coaching. The way a training organisation measures success is – not unreasonably – that they want students who have enrolled on a particular course to complete that course successfully. They want A = the number of students and B = the number of successful course completions, to be the same number, or as close to the same number as possible. What happens to coaches once they leave the course simply isn't the concern of the coaching course provider. Again, let me stress, that doesn't make them bad, it is reasonable of them to use that particular key performance indicator (KPI), they are training providers after all. They are no more responsible for what happens to you once you complete their course than your high school or university was.

However, what I know to be true, is that when coach training providers do teach business development, they teach it at a very superficial level. They often teach good basic business administration and client record management, but marketing is something of a black hole in the curriculum. Coaches I've spoken to tell me of marketing advice given to them on their course being about flyers and networking, and all of them were of the belief that all they needed to do was get the first few clients and the rest would come flooding via word of mouth.

What coach training providers offer rarely has enough marketing substance for the coach to be able to walk away and put it into practice. The evidence for this is of course, that 82% failure rate.

An Aside

Let's look at business development skills for a moment. We are not taught these skills at school. As an aside, I believe that in order to thrive in the 21st century that we should be teaching these skills in schools. I feel so strongly about this that I delivered a TEDx talk on the topic (if you search 'Sarah Short TEDx', you'll find it).

Even those who have taken a degree in business or marketing, tell me that they don't cover actual business development. They don't learn how to market and sell their own product or service. They don't leave university with the skills and knowledge they need to start their own business. In fact, a couple of our earliest mentees had degrees in business studies. In short, the entire education systems of the western world are designed to create employees, not entrepreneurs.

Talk to employees about sales and selling, and unless they're actually salespeople, they'll often shudder. To be honest, even for those who are salespeople, being a salesperson for the ACME organisation, who introduces themselves as *Sarah Short, from ACME Inc* is a whole different ball game and crucially *feels* completely different to introducing yourself as *Sarah Short from, well, Sarah Short Coaching*.

Most of us will come from cultures where salespeople are not held in high regard. We tend to think of them as slightly dodgy. There's something about the idea of selling that makes us hark back to the 1980s and 90s, and the nasty, high-pressure sales techniques of the time-share or second-hand car industries. I've been in sales for most of my career and I've can promise you that I have never, ever used a high-pressure sales technique. It isn't necessary.

Coaches however, tend to feel that somehow, selling coaching goes against the whole idea of coaching, and that's often why they don't like it. Coaching is about being client-centred and talking about coaching as a service and then adding in talking about money (yuk, right?) can make coaches feel unwell!

In this book, I'll show you how to grow your coaching business without having to feeling slimy or grubby. I'll clearly demonstrate how, with the right skills and knowledge, coaches can make the very best salespeople of all. Most of all, I'll show you that selling is simply good customer service.

Alisa Barcan – Case Study

Alisa is a chartered accountant, with an astonishing career in accounting for a woman of her tender years. She took a coaching diploma at Cambridge University and she came to the end of the diploma. She realised that although her coaching skills and her accounting skills were sound, she had no idea about business development.

What follows is Alisa in her own words, from an interview we had together.

Alisa's Background

My background is in chartered accountancy, I'm an accountant by profession. I've held several accountancy roles before moving into more commercial and analysis type roles a few years back. I love working with numbers and being able to read and tell the story behind the numbers was always my thing. It's something that I'm known for in the professional accounting world. Excel is one of my best friends. I've been called the Queen of Spreadsheets on more than one occasion!

In May 2017, I had a big birthday and as is often the case, I really started to question the impact that I was making in the world both as an individual and as a professional. I was in a very good job, working for a multinational company and doing very well at adding to their bottom line. This felt like a contradiction was because I didn't really feel that I was making enough of a difference to the world.

I wanted to be able to use my skills beyond improving the company's profit line. I wanted to impact individuals and to some extent I was already doing that, as I'd gradually started to help friends and family understand the way their money works. For example, I helped them to understand how tax works, and what the impact of their pension contributions is, and how to manage their finances in general. However, I wanted to extend my reach and be able to help other people as well.

After lots of soul – and internet – searching, I realised that what I was doing was similar to something called financial coaching. I started to read more about that, and finally deciding to do a financial coaching qualification. That was in September 2017, and a lot has happened since then!

The most important thing for me was that coaching gave me what I was looking for. I was looking to make a difference in people's lives. I haven't been coaching for very long, but the transformations that I have already been able to see in the lives of my clients are really, really rewarding and humbling. I have to pinch myself every day when I get the kind testimonial that says, "financial coaching has changed my life!".

How Alisa Found Us

Before I found The Coaching Revolution, I wasn't really doing much in terms of business development. I had only just started.

The business development part of my business at this point, was purely based on word of mouth. I would get new clients based on referrals from existing or previous clients.

I wasn't sure how to build my business, I searched for coaching jobs online, and then I found one of your articles on LinkedIn. That then led me to your website. I listened to a few podcasts, and I read a few blog posts. I started to relate to The Coaching Revolution without even knowing you as individuals. I had already chosen my mentor even before I had my first contact with you!

I joined The Coaching Revolution in April 2018, and that was right after I finished the first module of my coaching course with university. It dawned on me that although I *could* learn about running a business on my own and from courses and materials I could find online a) it would take me a lot of time, which I did not have at this point and b) it wouldn't really necessarily be tailored to the UK market. I wanted to work with someone who has done this before, who has made mistakes that I can learn from without having to go through the trial and error myself.

I didn't want to go down that route of doing a free course and then at the end of it, when I've had a bit of value, the trainer saying, "Well, in order to get real value now you have to pay for this." I would have wasted all my time doing that course just to get to the end of it and find out that the really good stuff – the stuff I needed – I would have had to pay for it anyway.

The one-to-one interaction was very important for me too. I didn't want to go and learn in a group. I knew that I wanted what I needed to learn to be tailored to my own needs. I really wanted a mentor that I could work with and who would be mine for the duration of my learning experience.

Once I found you, I took a practical step and did a cost-benefit analysis and it seemed to me that joining The Coaching Revolution was really worth it.

I contacted you, and then the magic happened!

What Have You Gained From The Coaching Revolution?

What I didn't realise at the time, was that I was actually joining a community. That meant that I would be interacting and learning from all of the members in that community, not just my mentor. That was one of the many bonuses that I got. What was particularly special was that within that community I found a safe space for me to practise my marketing message, and access to online training and other types of learning. Sharing knowledge and getting feedback from other coaches who are on the same journey as me has been so valuable. The community itself has been a really great bonus that I wasn't actually actively looking for, but it's been great to have.

On reflection, the community is probably the most important bit. I think that it's so easy when you work on your own, as coaches do, to sit behind a computer screen without having any interaction with people. The problem with that is that it can drive you mad. It's easy to get cabin fever from looking at the same four walls all day, and so I love our community for saving me, and all of us, from that.

What Was Your Biggest Challenge In The Work You Did With Us?

I think my biggest challenge was a mental challenge.

I'm a millennial and so I had this idea that the mentoring would be us discussing social media and search engine optimisation. I thought we'd talk about marketing campaigns and how to launch a product or service in order to attract more clients.

We did do some of that, but actually the approach to winning more business is much more simple than I thought, and it's this:

1. Know who you are. Be very clear on how you can serve your clients.
2. Know exactly who your clients are.
3. Know where they are and just get out there and talk to people about what you do.

The fact that this is so simple almost stopped me from doing it. I'm a fairly regimented person and I thought, *this can't be it! There has to be more to it than this!*

I think it's really easy to over-complicate things and to think that you need an army of tools to be successful, when actually what you need is a clear vision, and the time to implement it.

Getting my head around how simple this process is was actually quite challenging, in fact it was the most challenging thing for me. I didn't have any problems doing any of the technical work that my mentor asked me to do. But just the idea of these three things, I don't know. It sounded almost too good to be true.

I know that there's plenty of advice available that tells new coaches to subscribe to various platforms and packages and to spend lots of money on subscriptions. It's easy to end up spending £200 or more a month when actually, what you really need as a new coach, is paying clients. What I've just described, happens in all areas of life not just coaching. The fact that you throw money at something makes you think that you've done your job, and all you have to do now is wait and the clients will flood to you, which is not the case.

What's even more unfortunate is that these coaches usually belong to some online community or other of coaches (on Facebook perhaps), some of whom simply **must** have been through this before, but they don't say anything at all. They could be really helpful to new coaches by saying *hey, don't spend your money on pointless things when you could spend it somewhere else and get real value*, but they don't. I'm not sure why? Perhaps they feel foolish and don't want to share.

What Is The Best Thing About Working With The Coaching Revolution?

The best thing of all was the feedback and encouragement from my mentor Paul Snell. His ability to pick up clues, not so much from what I was saying, but from what I *wasn't* saying was flawless, and his ability to build on that is strong.

I'm a very diplomatic person, and I give situations the benefit of the doubt. I often won't immediately say something that's on my mind until I have mulled it over and done a cost-benefit analysis (or whatever). However, Paul was very quick to pick up on clues that I wasn't even aware that I was sending, and to quickly make me take action on those so that we could move on. His intuition was spot on and that's been great.

I've also made new friends in the community, and best of all is that they're on the same path as I am. They understand what I'm going through. We help each other and we can get to where we want to go faster because we work together. I really appreciate that.

There have also been some highlight moments that I've been able to share with everyone in our community. One example is that since Paul and I started working together, and I completely understood what my marketing message needed to be, I've been writing articles to support that message on LinkedIn. A couple of these have been selected for publication on global media outlets; Thrive Global and The Financial Diet, as well as the Harvard Business Review. That feels amazing!

How Do You Feel About The Future?

I feel very positive about the future. When I started my mentoring with The Coaching Revolution, my offering was one-to-one coaching, but now I'm discussing with my mentor how to offer workshops and training. I also have a one-year goal to penetrate the corporate market and start working with organisations so that I can reach as many people and help them improve their financial situation.

I'm really excited and very positive about the future.

What Advice Would You Give To Those Who Are Thinking Of Working With Us?

I would ask them this: *What's stopping you?*

There might be several things, maybe they need more clarity in terms of what they can expect to get. I hope that this interview answered some of those questions, but of course they should talk to you Sarah, to clarify things further.

I think for a lot of people, it's the money element – the price – that they worry about, and that just happens to be my speciality! Let me explain the approach that I had when I did my own calculations in my cost-benefit analysis:

The prices that The Coaching Revolution charge are, on a per-hour basis, very similar to what many coaches might charge for a single coaching session. If a person as a coach is not willing to invest this kind of money for their own development as a business owner, then I think they're very unlikely to be comfortable to charge that amount for their own services.

It's a matter of mindset more than anything else. If you get butterflies thinking about working with The Coaching Revolution, can I point out that this is *exactly* what you should be feeling. If this is a stretch for you, then it means that you'll put more effort into making it work. Of course, as a financial coach I understand that a lot of people have budget constraints, but at the same time it's amazing how creative and resourceful people become when they really want something.

My advice in a nutshell is to understand very clearly what you will get as a mentee, and if that's something that you know you need in your business, then make it happen. Chances are that you will need to do it anyway at some point, so you will only be wasting time and effort and money if you delay.

Do it now!

What You DON'T Need to Do to Grow a Coaching Business

This is a quick and sneaky chapter to tell you what I believe that you don't need in order to start a business. It's so short it doesn't deserve the title of 'chapter' but it's important enough not to be tied to some other chapter.

Coaches who come from an employed, corporate or business background are used to structure. They have grown up in it both educationally and then career-wise. When they decide to create a coaching business, coaches with this type of background often take the same first steps.

Whilst they don't actually try to duplicate the corporate structure, they certainly feel that they need to have 'structure' present. Often that structure includes a limited company, branding and a website. Let me state quite clearly and for the record, that you absolutely and definitely do not need those things to start your coaching business.

You don't need a limited company, you don't need a website, or branding, or logos or any of those things. What you need, is paying clients.

Limited Company

A limited company is a private company whose owners are legally responsible for its debts only to the extent of the amount of capital they invested. So if you set up a limited company with 10 shares of £1 each and you own them all, your liability for the company's debts is limited to £10. In contrast, a sole-trader is responsible for all debts that they accrue.

A limited company is a legal entity and the director(s) have certain legal obligations that they must fulfil – most of them relating to accounts.

If you're going to be working with corporations, then it may be that you need to begin with a limited company for credibility. Otherwise, it's a headache that you are probably best avoiding in the beginning.

People who are coaches and come from a corporate background like limited companies, because it feels like structure and structure feels safe. However, you **do not** need a limited company to be open for business.

Website

This is the single biggest waste of money a coach can fall foul of. Until you know what kind of clients you're going to be working with and what they need to hear, you don't need a website. In fact, you actually don't want one.

There are countless coaching websites out there with gorgeous (and expensive) photos of the coach and lists of what they can do, and how much they charge. What they don't do is articulate why a client should work with them. (Spoiler alert; clients don't care about your coaching experience and qualifications anywhere near as much as you do!)

The best single tip for a new coach that will save them the most in terms of resources (time, energy and/or money) is to avoid having a website to start with. Leave it until your coaching business has enough income to pay for one, because then – and only then – you'll know what it needs to say.

If you're thinking of creating a homemade website, may I please discourage you from doing so? Make no mistake, a poor and clearly homemade website is more damaging to you than no website at all. Conversely, don't spend your money on having a fancy website in the early days when a) you don't know what it needs to say yet and b) what you really need is paying clients.

I promise you, no one is searching for you, or indeed any other coach, on Google. Nor are they going to land on your website by accident and decide to buy from you. I reiterate, wait until you know what you're doing before you spend money on a website.

Branding

You don't need branding, or a fancy business name to start getting paying clients. Branding, whilst enormously fun to play with, is unnecessary at the beginning of your journey to create a financially viable coaching business.

Why You WANT These Things!

The thing about branding, and websites and limited companies is that creating them makes you feel like you're working. The countless hours that we can spend messing around with colour and fonts, with images and webpages make us think we've worked hard on our business. I don't mean to disparage here – you will have worked damned hard, but it won't be moving you in the direction you want it to; that direction being acquiring paying clients.

Those hours we spend make us feel like we're doing good things and that we've put in a good day's work towards starting our businesses. However, that's a false premise. What you really need to be doing is generating enquiries from people who understand what you do and want to work with you.

Shall we begin?

Becoming Bilingual

Coaches are positive, forward looking folk. We don't dwell; we accept, we brush off and we move on. We take responsibility for our actions and our lives.

When we work with our clients, we get them to look past the problems, the pitfalls and the issues to a brighter future that they can create and then reach. We don't encourage our clients to have a pity-party with every little thing that goes wrong, we encourage them to see negatives as bumps in the road.

This is the work of a coach.

We can describe our work and talk about it with other coaches. We talk about *goals, limiting beliefs, breakthroughs, mental barriers etc.* You will speak this language fluently, all coaches do. I call it 'coach-speak' and it's our mother-tongue. It talks of coaching focus, and coaching outcomes.

We **want** to talk about goals and achieving them; about mental barriers and recognising them; about limiting beliefs and removing them. However, the sad truth is that our potential clients don't care about those things. Let's face it, no one knows that they have a limiting belief until it's revealed to them, do they? Before that moment, the limiting belief is simply their truth.

Coach-Speak -v- Client-Speak

Marketing language is different from coaching language. Marketing language has to be language that the clients we want to attract can hear and understand. Let me repeat that, because it's important. *Marketing language has to be the language that the clients we want to attract can hear and understand.*

What do I mean? Well, coaches tend to want to talk in coach-speak, because it's our language. Coaching is focused on outcomes, but marketing needs to be focused on problems and potential solutions and that, dear reader, is the big stumbling block that coaches face. Marketing needs to be in a language other than coach-speak. It needs to be in client-speak.

In short, coaches need to be bilingual.

Do you remember Worzel Gummidge? He was a character from a children's story, a scarecrow that could change heads as required in order to deal with different situations (serious head, comedy head, posh head, hardworking head... you get the idea?).

Coaches need two heads. We need our 'coach head', that talks coach-speak but we also need our 'marketing head' that talks client-speak. Understand this; having those two heads mean that we **can** be bilingual.

What's Client-Speak?

Client-speak is laser-focused language that cuts through the nonsense and gets right to the heart of the biggest problem that the client you want to work with has.

Client-speak says *I know you have this problem; I know how it affects your whole life, I can show you how your life could look without it and I can clearly demonstrate that I understand the whole situation*. It also says *I can help you, why don't we talk?* in a way that makes a potential client want to engage with you.

Coaches flinch about using marketing-speak, because it seems to directly conflict with coach-speak. However, if we remember those two heads (and my weighing scale analogy of earlier) we can see that actually, coaches need both heads, and both sets of language, to thrive in business.

The gap in a coach's understanding of how to use those two different sorts of language accounts for the (previously mentioned) global statistic that says that 82% of coaching businesses will fail. **That's** how important it is to be bilingual in your business.

Client-speak gets the client in front of you in the first place, coach-speak keeps them there.

Different Dialects In Client-Speak

If all clients spoke the same language, then it would be really easy to attract enquiries from potential clients. Sadly, that's not the way that the world works. Each kind of ideal client speaks their own dialect; their own version of client-speak.

A person coming up to retirement who is ripe for some coaching to help them to overcome their anxiety around the uncertainty facing them, speaks a different language than, say, the mum who wants to start a business to fit in with her children. Yes, they both need to set goals, to overcome some limiting beliefs and to remove some mental barriers, but a) they don't know that and b) they have such different aspirations and worries that trying to talk to them with the same kind of client-speak is clearly not going to be productive.

Once you know who your ideal client is, you will understand what dialect they speak. It will become increasingly clear to you exactly what you need to say, how to say it and where to say it. Your efforts to date, which have almost certainly involved casting your net wide, probably haven't yielded the results you're looking for, or you wouldn't be reading this book.

Together, we're going to learn client-speak. In particular, we're going to learn the version of client-speak that your future clients speak. You will be able to speak the words that your potential clients need to hear in order to understand exactly why they should work with you.

Imagine that! Potential clients who come to you with an issue that they want to resolve and already understand that you can help them!

Not Just A Load Of Old Codswallop!

I hope you've realised by now that this idea of becoming bilingual isn't just a load of old codswallop! It's the single most important thing that you can do to market your coaching business.

Part of becoming bilingual is deducing which version of client-speak you need to master and that, dear coach, is entirely dependent upon who your ideal client is.

Three Steps To Success

There are three steps to success in marketing your coaching business. They are each very simple, but as I'll no doubt say many times before our time together is done, that doesn't mean that they're easy. Let's face it, if they were easy then every single coach would have a financially viable coaching business, wouldn't they? And that 82% is lingering around like a bad smell, reminding us that they don't.

1. The first step is identifying your own personal ideal client.
2. The second step is working out what that kind of client needs to hear from you in order to have the lightbulb moment that goes like this: *they're talking about me!*
3. The third step is figuring out where this kind of client is, both on and offline.

In some ways, online is the easy one. It's 2020 and we're all familiar with social media. We're often much less familiar with where people hang out in the real world. Having an ideal client means that you'll know.

Sarah Gilligan – Case Study

Australian coach Sarah Gilligan has a background in the creative industry. With a hugely diverse freelance career that has included stage management, TV production and circus management, Sarah found coaching when she was working as a business development manager for the Australian Centre for Dialogue.

What follows is Sarah in her own words, from an interview we had together.

Sarah's Background

When I first started overhearing coaches talking at the Australian Centre for Dialogue, my antenna started twitching. I was listening to the language they used, and the topics that they were talking about and I realised that this was very similar to the language and topics I'd learned when training to be a stage manager.

There are a lot of things about how we get in touch with our humanity that happen in a rehearsal room, that also happen in a coaching conversation. They are both about connecting, and participating, and I heard what they were saying, and I wanted in.

I had reached a point where I had to do something else with my life, because I no longer could work a 10-hour day. I'd ended up with chronic fatigue, but my bread and butter job was in the film industry which means a 10-hour minimum day. I couldn't carry on. It just wasn't an option anymore. I had been looking for something else, and I found it in coaching. I went and got an ICF coaching qualification, I finished my training and I thought *I don't know what to do now*.

What Were You Doing Regarding Business Development Before You Found The Coaching Revolution?

I was completely obsessed with making this work because this is it for me, this is what I want to do for the rest of my life. I've finally found it.

What I was doing before I found you, was trying things out. I was being very proactive in my marketing. I'd never been on social media before, it just didn't interest me, but I realised that I needed to be on social media to market a coaching business. I tried a whole lot of different things, I put out everything I could think of, even a 2-for-1 offer for the New Year. I got heaps of clients coming in the door at the beginning of the year. Somebody that I was speaking to at the time went, "Gosh! Whatever you're doing is working." I was delighted.

But, of course, they were people from my world, and whilst those people from my world needed my help, they could only afford it when I was offering it for half of a very cheap price. However, even then, after a couple of sessions, they just couldn't afford it anymore. I suddenly found that I had all of these people that I was halfway through a coaching journey with. I started coaching them for free, because I didn't feel that I could just leave them. It wasn't a great situation.

I was starting to believe that the creative sector, one with which I have great affinity, wasn't a sector that could afford coaching. These are the people that I want to help. I think that a coaching culture would be exceptionally good in the creative industry, because it is a process that is a creative process after all. In fact, I'm amazed that the creative industry isn't inundated with coaches, but it isn't.

I started to think who could afford to pay for coaching and I decided to go for wealthy women who are bit of a crossroads and if it's people from, say the IT industry, I didn't care anymore. I decided that I want to coach so much that I can compromise. I wanted to work with women heading for burnout as I felt that this was a place where coaching would be beneficial and I decided that I was going to change what I was doing and to market myself in this space, as that's a much bigger market and thought I could tap into it.

I started to change all the work I'd put in so far. On my website for example, everything that I'd done I'd set up very specifically for the creative sector. I started pulling all of that out and making it much more generic. I stated that I put 20% of my profits towards helping people in the creative sector (and I really do by the way) because the mental health and wellbeing of the creative sector is core to my business. I felt like I was still doing what I was meant to be doing, but now I was flapping around here and there a bit and just started feeling lost.

I wasn't getting the results I wanted from my marketing efforts and it felt like the minute I took my foot off the pedal (and I was putting in an incredible amount of effort to just try and rally a single client) it all stopped.

I'd reached a point where a creative sector contact had said to me that the industry was *crying out* for what I could offer. I knew there was a need, I just had no idea how to tap into it. I knew where I wanted to go, but I didn't trust myself and my ability to play in that world where people look at you blankly when you talk about coaching. They just don't know what that word means.

I was a bit scared. I've always been someone who just wings my way through things. I'm very much a 'let's just do something, get it out there, see what works and keep things moving' kind of person, but I felt really, really strangled by not knowing what the right thing to do was or who to trust to advise me.

I'd picked up a few free strategy sessions with people who said that they helped coaches find clients. I think the worst one, was when I had a really long conversation with somebody who I felt was such a con man. However, I found myself agreeing to an expensive programme he was running. I paid by credit card and woke up in the night feeling sick. I sent him a message the following day telling him I wanted out and he was so abusive! I think I dodged a bullet there. The thing is, for coaches who need help, it's an absolute minefield out there.

These people are legion, and they all have cookie-cutter solutions to marketing that just don't work. If they did, more coaches would be making a living. I think it's really unethical, yet I know that there are a lot of people out there who are preying on new coaches.

In the end, I'd downloaded enough paid stuff that was supposed to be helpful that the money I spent was getting close to what I'd paid for my credential. It was insane, it was contradictory, and it didn't work!

I was lost.

How Did You Find The Coaching Revolution?

I saw the advertisement for the webinar series you did for the ICF Australasia chapter. It was about how to define an ideal client and I thought 'that sounds like *just* what I need to do!'

I think I was in the middle of a big mess of thinking, should I be aiming at creative people? Should I just think about working with women? Then I thought that suddenly lots of men seem to want my coaching, so I was in the middle of all of that confusion and saw the webinar ad and thought, 'Oh my God! Brilliant! Let's do that'.

Anyway, I got a heap out of the webinar. However, I was in such a mess that I didn't roll with the information straight away. I didn't quite trust it because I'd been burned before.

I made my ideal client avatar, but I didn't quite believe her. I was at a place where I was questioning how specific you said I needed to be. I found myself thinking but *why* does it have to be a man OR a woman? Why can't it be anybody who...?

I missed the point, which is odd, because I knew the point. I knew the point because I spent my life in storytelling and that's what we do through your process. It's great. However, I went off and thought that I could do it all myself for a bit longer and then was just starting to get more and more desperate. I'd connected with you on LinkedIn and there was a rapport that we had. I thought *I like everything about what she's doing and saying*.

I'd reached the point where I needed to decide which voice I trusted in the noise. I saw something about becoming a mentee and it was just the perfect time for me, so I committed to it. Well, the rest is a quick juggernaut to being here.

What Were You Hoping To Get From The Coaching Revolution?

A way to get decent paying clients and some clarity. And just one voice to listen to, I was sick of trying to figure out who was talking sense and who wasn't.

However, the beautiful thing about The Coaching Revolution is that it isn't just one voice. For example, on the weekly Monday night sessions, there are a variety of voices and they've all got different areas of expertise which is really interesting. It feels very carefully curated, which it is of course. What I've experienced is that I've come in and I've got trust. I've got trust with a group of people who know what I'm going through, and what needs to happen to change that.

If I point out here that the Monday night webinars are actually UK time, so they are 5:30am Tuesday morning for me, and I get up to join in as often as I can. When you consider that I love my sleep, that says something about how valuable they are, doesn't it? I'm also not the only Australian who attends them. They're great.

What's also important is that The Coaching Revolution is a place where I feel totally safe to just be where I am, and to take what I want at different times. I can ask questions. I can find my own way of working through the program and the process, but with the support and ideas of other people as well.

The International Coach Federation (ICF) does offer a lot of really fantastic stuff around business development, but it's not the same as working with somebody who is available throughout the week. For example when you're writing an email to somebody to pitch something, you might want some feedback on it before you send it, and The Coaching Revolution mentors can help you with that in a reasonable timescale, because they've seen it all before and done it too. I needed some help with workshop design and you immediately gave me access to Kathryn MacNeill, your 'workshop design queen' who I can now go and work with when I need her. It's things like program design, workshop design, all of these things that just don't come into the basic marketing training that others offer.

Remember, I was paralyzed by the number of different voices out there saying that they had the best ideas and advice for making this or that happen, for me getting inbound clients, for me getting clarity about how I take my next steps.

However, with you guys I took the first step and began creating my ideal client avatar. At first, I approached it like an academic exercise. I thought I could see the value of it. However, then you said to me that I wasn't trying to write an essay, and that I should consider that I was actually writing a story. Most importantly, you pointed out that my ideal client doesn't have to be a real someone that I actually know. When I realised that I didn't have to know this person already, suddenly it became fun! I found a whole untapped well of knowledge that I had about my ideal client that I simply hadn't realised was there. A torrent was unleashed!

What Did You Get From The Coaching Revolution?

I've got my enthusiasm back for my coaching business, that's HUGE!

The really good thing is that I got my commitment back to the arts, and to the creative sector and to helping the women in that industry and I've got an actual path to getting me there. It's been incredible for me. I'm feeling relieved, supported, looked after and inspired and I get to write, and to play with you, and that's all fantastic. I have my energy back, and my motivation. In short, life looks good again on the coaching front.

What did you discover that was unexpected?

Unexpected? Well that has to be the gaps in knowledge that I had.

My whole life, I've been someone who's been able to make it up as I go along. I've always volunteered to do things that are well outside of my comfort zone, and just barrelled on in there and made it happen – whatever 'it' was. I've always had strong opinion about things and working with The Coaching Revolution made me realise that there's a difference between an opinion and knowledge.

I started to realise that they are actually just gaps in my knowledge. I now know that there are people out there – ones that that I am now connected to – who have that knowledge and I just need to get it. More importantly, it's not as scary as I thought.

Yes, the unexpected thing was definitely realising how much I actually didn't know. It's that whole conscious conscientiousness thing. I realised that I had a lot further to go with my business development than I thought I had.

How do you feel about the future?

Excited about my coaching business. Excited with a level of confidence that's clearly making a difference. There are all sorts of 'ooky, spooky things' going off now since I nailed my avatar. I now have somebody hosting a Boltcutter evening with a group of women who fit my ICA. (Boltcutter is the name of my coaching business).

With Kathryn's help I have a workshop designed and I've got all of these things that are just suddenly started landing all at once. Isn't that just the way life goes? Once you know what you're doing, opportunities start to appear...

Whereas before I was just out there in the killing field, just flapping around with a whole lot of other coaches who are also stuck. That's the whole thing. It's not a regulated industry. I've fought the term life coaching for a very long time because I'd always thought that life coaching sounded hippie 'right out there' stuff. But it turns out that actually, there are a whole lot of things about the coaching industry that are so misunderstood. For example, it's hard to know what to call yourself when you're a coach, but I'm working on it. For a few years when I was working a lot around dialogue and the social enterprise stuff, but I was also working in film and I had five different emails addresses and I just called myself Sarah Gilligan, Enthusiastic Participant in the World. That's good, isn't it?

What would you say to those who might be thinking about working with us?

Just do it. Just start the process.

A conversation with Sarah is one of those strategy calls, one of those offerings that is well worth picking up. This is one of the quality ones. Don't mess around in that pool for as long as I did.

Perhaps everyone has to go through that 'lost' thing? It might be just like a rite of passage or something new coaches have to do? I hope not, when they could avoid it all by working with you.

The Ideal Client

In this chapter, I'm going to explain why having an ideal client avatar (ICA) is utterly essential for a coaching business to thrive. I'm also going to talk about why you don't believe me. Honestly, you don't have to believe me, but I can promise you that you're far more likely to be one of the 1 in 5 coaches that do succeed if you take my word for it.

Can I just stop for a moment and explode a myth? This ICA that I'm talking about isn't a niche. This ICA-is-the-same-thing-as-a-niche myth can cause real issues, so let me explain the difference.

Imagine a funnel. The wide-open end of the funnel. the top of it, would be your niche. For example, a niche could be men in technology, or women in business. The bottom end of that funnel, the tiny hole at the bottom, is where the ideal client is found.

In the cases of those niches of men in technology or women in business, the ideal client within that first niche might be Fred Bloggs, aged 42, 6'1'' tall, married with 3 kids. He's been in a middle management role for 10 years and wants to move into senior management. The ideal client for the other niche might be Jane Doe, aged 38, 5'2'' with 2 children under 5 years of age. She was a marketing professional before she had her children and fully intended to return to work after her maternity leave. However, once her children were born, her priorities and values changed and she realised that actually, she wants to be home more, because she wants to be the one to bring up her children.

The lack of detail in a niche makes it a good starting point. The incredible detail of an ICA will make it your whole marketing effort easier. Make no mistake, understanding who you are speaking to in your marketing, as well as what they need to hear, will make everything you do have a purpose. That purpose is to make you visible to your client.

Counterintuitive

An ICA is the outline of the kind of individual with whom you want to work; your perfect coaching client. It is one fictitious individual who embodies these people. They are the client that makes your heart sing when you know you're going to be seeing them today. They understand the value that your coaching offers them, and they are happy to pay your fees, without quibbling, in order to get that value. They take the actions they agree to in each coaching session and come to the next one with renewed vigour and enthusiasm. They are truly your ideal client. If your coaching diary was full of these perfect clients, not only would you be making the income you want, you'd be doing it with a very glad heart. Add to that the fact that you'd be the one in five who actually make this coaching gig work. Your business would be not only emotionally fulfilling, but financially fulfilling too.

Once your ICA is defined, all your marketing, *all of it,* is focused on this person. Everything you write, say or do marketing-wise, is aimed at this one person. Having an ICA makes all of your marketing simple; you can pre-plan it, schedule it for social media and you'll always know the right thing to say to attract exactly the kind of client that you want.

It sounds too good to be true, doesn't it? I'm delighted to tell you that is isn't. Remember, that your perfect client doesn't know you exist yet. They are not searching for you. Having a website for them to find is a pointless effort if they're not actually looking for you in the first place, isn't it? Having your ICA nailed is the thing that will make you visible. That's what you need to become; visible. Not visible to the whole world, just visible to your ideal client.

Vanilla Marketing

When I talk to groups of coaches and I ask them who they work with, if they start to answer with the words *anyone who,* I know that they don't have clients. Let me explain why.

In this 21st century world of marketing noise, we are continually bombarded with marketing messages. Apparently, we see more than 3000 of these messages a day!

Not only do we see advertisements on the television, hear them on the radio and see them on billboards and in magazines and newspapers as we always did, we are also receiving marketing messages via social media too. If you think of your Facebook feed, it's littered with the stuff your friends and family post, but it also has a number of sponsored posts. Sponsored posts are advertisements and the reason that you see the ones you see isn't an accident, it's because you fit their ideal client profile.

LinkedIn and Instagram are the same. Snapchat and Pinterest are no different either. Advertising (which is simply a form of marketing) is everywhere. If we click on something that caught our interest, we'll find that suddenly, advertisements for that product or service seems to appear all over the place. Facebook tracks what you do when you're not using their platform, so that they can use any actions you take online, to offer you targeted advertising when you return. Amazon will offer you things it thinks you may like, based on your previous purchases and it will suggest, all the way to the checkout, things that other people who bought what you're buying also liked.

Have you ever found yourself watching an advertisement on the television and wondering what on earth they're going on about? The message that they're sending is simply not getting through to you? Guess what, they don't care, because you're not their ideal client. The people who are most likely to buy from them will understand exactly what they're talking about, and that's what they're aiming for. They are prepared to lose you as a potential customer in order to make sure that the person most likely to buy from them will hear their message and understand it. The reason that they're prepared to lose you, is that you probably wouldn't have bought from them anyway. This is going to become much less common as we move online more and more. The ads we see online are carefully targeted for us, so they will all make sense to us.

Focused Marketing

As consumers, we have developed a very keen ability to ignore most of the marketing we see. We barely even notice it. If it isn't directly relevant to us, we simply don't see it. Let me say that again; if it isn't directly relevant to us, we simply don't see it. What I'm saying here is that marketing, all effective marketing, is targeted.

Large organisations have ideal clients. Companies like Virgin, Apple, and Microsoft have ideal clients. They target their marketing at the people who are most likely to benefit from what they're selling, because those are the people who are most likely to buy.

The Virgin travel company has three ICAs; the lone adventurer, the business traveller and those taking family holidays. If you don't belong to one of those three groups, you are very welcome to buy from them, but they're not going to market to you. You are not on their radar when it comes to marketing, but they'll happily take your money from you should you wish to purchase a flight from them.

As a coach, you probably feel that you have lots of perfect clients. You want to work with (for example) the young professional, looking to advance in their career; you are also interested in coaching those moving into management and leadership; while you're at it, you would be very interested in coaching executives who are struggling with work/life balance. You have lots of ICAs, right?

To build your business, you need to focus on one ICA and generate a solid income stream from that one. Virgin has a multi-million-pound (dollar) marketing budget, so they can have entire separate marketing teams working on each of their ICAs. You don't have that budget (if you do, why are you reading this book and not working 1:1 with us? It's a much faster route to success, and it won't cost a million either!).

What I'm trying to say is that you need to focus your marketing towards your ICA. You can sell coaching to anyone you want to. If someone enquires and they're not even close to fitting your ICA, you don't have to send them packing. You, just like Virgin, are free to **sell** to whomsoever you want.

Why You Don't Believe Me

The idea of having an ICA doesn't make rational sense to people who are new to the concept. Why on earth would you focus all your time and energy to marketing to one type of client, even if that client is a 'perfect' client? Surely, in doing that, you're missing out on the opportunities that exist to coach the other 7 billion people on the planet, right? It simply **has** to make more sense to market to *anyone who...*

To reiterate what I said a few paragraphs ago, people don't hear marketing that isn't directly aimed at them. That's why no matter how often coaches use their marketing to talk about removing limiting beliefs, or mental barriers, about reaching goals and overcoming procrastination, it doesn't work. The clients that they imagined might think *I have limiting beliefs! I want to reach goals!* simply aren't there.

Let me tell you why: No one cares!

The Sad Truth

No one gives two hoots about limiting beliefs, mostly because they don't actually realise they have them. If we knew we had limiting beliefs, they wouldn't be limiting beliefs, right? Limiting beliefs are just part of the fabric of who we are. If you remember the Jim Carey film *The Truman Show,* limiting beliefs are like the dome he lived in. He thought it was the 'real world', until he discovered it wasn't. Coaching reveals limiting beliefs, but the person who is being coached didn't know that those beliefs were there, until they were exposed.

No one cares about goals much either. If I could have a penny for every coaching client of mine who has said *I have no idea how to set a goal, because I have no idea what I want* I could, well, buy a nice slice of cake and decent cup of coffee at least.

I realise that what I've just said goes against everything we coaches believe. Coaching is **all about** removing limiting beliefs and helping clients reach goals, after all. However, we're not talking about coaching, we're talking about the business of coaching and those two things, are, as I've said before, very different things.

If I ask a coach what they do, they'll usually try and define coaching for me. They'll tell me about removing limiting beliefs, they'll tell me that they help people reach their goals and dreams. Have you ever noticed what happens to someone who asks a coach what they do, when they themselves have no idea what coaching is? I'll tell you. They glaze over after the first three sentences. The coach can wax lyrical about coaching techniques and the person they're talking to is frantically looking round the room for a means of escape.

Coaching clients don't buy the coaching process. Coaching clients buy the outcome. (I realise that what I wrote then is just a couple of sentences in a book full of them. However, should you choose to just remember only a few of my sentences, please make sure that these two make that list?)

Not buying a coaching process isn't remarkable, because actually, it's what we all do all the time. We don't buy insurance; we buy the peace of mind of knowing that if anything goes wrong, we're covered. We don't buy diet foods; we buy the feeling of getting into a pair of jeans a size smaller than we're in now. We don't buy nice golf clubs; we buy the reduction in our handicap that they'll give us. You see what I mean, right?

The coaching client is no different. They don't care about the coaching process. In fact, most of the time they know nothing about the coaching process. What they want is the outcome. That young professional wants the promotion; that new manager wants to feel that they know what they're doing and they're not going to be hated by their new team; the executive wants to be able to spend more time at home, or on the golf course. None of them particularly want coaching, it's simply a means to an end. Of course, once they have actually experienced coaching, this changes. But right now, we're talking about marketing and what that means is that we're talking about you as a coach generating some interest from those who may want to work with you. They're not your clients yet!

As I've said before, and I'll say again before our time together is through, the important thing to remember is that you need to be known for **one** thing. You need to sell **one** thing, to **one** client. Let me remind you again, this isn't forever, it's for *now*. You don't have to only ever coach one kind of person around one topic, but *you have to start somewhere*.

Creating Your Ideal Client

Creating an ICA is a chunky piece of work. I'm going to explain to you what you need to do, and why. Let me start by introducing you to The Coaching Revolution's ideal client avatar.

Meet Stella

Stella Hewitson is 42 and she qualified as a coach 10 years ago. She has a background in HR, which is how she discovered coaching (and got qualified) in the first place. Stella is married and has two children, aged 8 and 6. Stella has been trying to create a coaching business as a side-hustle for two years. Stella was quite sure that she knew what she was doing, as her confidence in her coaching ability was very strong.

In the beginning of her journey to creating a coaching business, Stella got busy. She registered a limited company and paid both a graphic designer and website creator for their talents. She has a lovely looking website that tells anyone who lands there who she is, what she's done, all about her coaching qualification and what kind of coaching she enjoys. It's been there for a couple of years, and honestly, even though it's never brought her any business, it's very professional-looking and Stella is very pleased with it.

Once her branding was in place, Stella created a few coaching programmes. By programmes, I mean different price points based on how many sessions of coaching the client wanted to commit to at the outset. Stella felt that a set price for a single session, with a discount for 6 sessions and a larger discount for 10 was fair.

Stella wants to work with anyone who feels 'stuck'. Those people who feel that they're not getting the most out of life, maybe because they haven't ever set themselves goals and then broken them down into milestones. Basically, they haven't ever been coached.

Once her programmes were created, Stella started a Facebook page and an Instagram account and set off to get some clients. She posts regularly. She is particularly fond of inspirational quotes, and so she got really good at creating memes. Memes are those lovely images, with quotes written on them, usually in some beautiful, flowing font. Stella posted religiously on Mondays, Wednesdays and Fridays, because she felt that they were the best days for inspiration; the beginning of the week, the middle and the end. She took her meme creation and quote finding very seriously and she now has hundreds of them in her library of resources.

Interestingly, although her friends all 'liked' her Facebook page, and they always liked the memes she shared, the memes didn't generate the interest that she expected. In fact, she didn't get a single paying coaching client from quite a lot of effort.

To recap; Stella's website doesn't bring in any clients, nor does her social media activity.

Stella's life is busy because she has a young family. She is still very disciplined about posting on social media 3 times a week and spends a couple of hours on a Sunday evening, crafting memes for the week. However, not one paying client has ever emerged from this activity.

Stella wants to ramp up her marketing for her coaching business, because she now needs this coaching business to become her source of income going forward. However, she really isn't sure **how**.

Stella's joined one of the myriad free Facebook groups for coaches and has become completely overwhelmed by a) all the talk of sales funnels and lead magnets etc (what on earth are they?) and b) the number of other coaches who offer their services, at a fee, to help her grow her business; they are legion!

She did find a great sounding online programme, offered in a sponsored Facebook ad from a bit of a guru that she followed and she spent nearly £1k on an online course. She found the course a bit difficult to follow because there were bits that didn't seem to apply to her business, or even to coaching so she didn't finish the course. Actually, that she spent that money at all is a bit of a guilty secret that Stella didn't tell her husband about. Stella feels a bit of a fool about having spent the money on what now seems to be a poor, generic marketing course.

As you can see, Stella has money to spend on acquiring knowledge, she just doesn't know where to go to spend it!

Stella lies awake at 3am, knowing that if she can't make this coaching business pay, then not only will she have wasted thousands of pounds on websites etc, but she won't be able to do the thing she loves; coaching.

Stella *loves* coaching, and really wants to build her coaching business. She would be delighted to spend several days a week working on it, *if only she knew what to do!*

Get The Idea?

Do you see how well I know Stella? I know what she's tried, I know how much she wants to coach for a living, and I know she has hit a brick wall in terms of how to make her coaching business work. She just wants to coach, and she simply can't figure out what she's doing wrong.

I could have said, that our niche is 'people who have a coaching qualification' and that would be true. I could have said that our niche is 'all coaches who want to have their own coaching business' and that would also be true. However, knowing those niches doesn't help us with our marketing, knowing Stella Hewitson certainly does.

But Why?

I can feel you asking 'why?'. Why does understanding the – frankly irrelevant – minutiae of Stella's life help?

As the person responsible for all the business development for The Coaching Revolution, I created Stella and I'm going to show you how to create your own version of her too. The reason she helps me so much is that she gives a focus to my marketing. Instead of saying 'we can help you to build a business' or even 'we help coaches to build businesses', we can be far more targeted with our language.

In our marketing, I can talk about how tricky it can be to build a coaching business while Stella is working full-time and bringing up a family. I can talk about why we're different from the charlatans I've mentioned before and why Stella can trust us. I can explain that our mentoring sessions can fit around her routines and that she doesn't have to worry about adding something else into her busy daytime. I can also talk specifically about how we can help her make a coaching business work, that she doesn't have to give up the dream of a coaching business, that she's not being thick it's just that she simply doesn't know what the right thing to do is. All of the marketing content I produce is aimed at Stella. All of it. I even wrote this book for Stella.

Here's the thing. Not one of our mentees (paying clients), is exactly like Stella. We have a couple of mentees who are quite close (and many more who are not) but not one of them is exactly like her. They all booked calls with me because they saw something in what I said that resonated with them, and their situation. Many of the conversations that I have with potential clients starts with them saying these words *I read something you wrote, and you were talking about me!* That sentence, from the mouths of potential clients, is the holy grail. It is exactly what you want to hear.

It's About Marketing, Not Selling

Your ICA is about who you will market to, not who you will sell to. I know I've said it before and I can promise you, I'll say it again before this book is done, because it is very important that you understand what I mean by this.

Imagine a dart board. Stella Hewitson is, for us, the bullseye. Your ICA will be your bullseye. If you throw a dart at a board and you miss the bullseye, there are still many other scores you can make; in fact, you can make more scores that *aren't* the bullseye than are, and so it is with your ICA marketing. You can, and will, sell your coaching to people who don't match your ideal client. In fact, it's rare to find a client who *exactly* matches them, and that's ok. What happens in the real world is that you will find clients who have a lot in common with your ICA, rather than being exact copies. Rather than being bullseyes on the dartboard, they are the scores around the bullseye and they're still worth points.

The reason you have an ICA is to enable your version of Stella, and those who struggle with the same issues that she does, to hear your marketing in the noise.

If you imagine scrolling through your Facebook feed on your phone, you kind of push your finger up the screen to scroll, right? Well, what we are all trying to do with our marketing is to get that scrolling person to STOP. The only way to do this is to make sure that what you've written, that they're reading, is *relevant.* If it's generic 'dream big and you will achieve' stuff, they won't stop. If it is aimed at 'anyone who…' they won't stop. If it says *hey, Stella, I get you! I know what you're struggling with and I CAN HELP* then they'll stop and engage. That engagement is the first step to gaining a client.

I hope this makes all things ICA clearer?

Coaching Versus Marketing

We all know that coaching isn't about telling. Coaching doesn't come from a place of the coach's knowledge at all. Coaching focuses on the client and is completely client-led.

Marketing on the other hand is about telling. You need to think about what problems you can help the client to solve.

People buy for one of two reasons; to either solve a problem or to fulfil a need. With coaching they buy to solve a problem. Honestly, in the initial stages of becoming a client, the client doesn't care about the vehicle – the coaching – all they care about is finding a solution to their problem. You, my dear coach, need to make sure that you are very clear about both the problem the client has and the solution that you can provide.

Creating Your ICA

You are going to create your own ideal client avatar now. You're going to create this perfect client, that you'll love to work with, and you're going to make them real; to you anyway. Let's get started!

If you already have coaching clients: Think of your favourite coaching clients – the ones you think 'yes!' when you see their names in your diary; the ones you really like working with. What do they have in common?

On a page, list every single common trait. (Demographic ones: age, marital status, income, gender, where they work, what industry they work in etc. Then move to things like beliefs, values, interests, lifestyle etc.).

If you think *but they're all **utterly** different!* then let's start with the fact that they're all human and go from there. There **will** be things that they have in common and your job is to find them.

If you're a brand-new coach: A good place to start is a younger version of yourself. How did you find coaching? What made you want to be coached? What problems were you facing that you couldn't solve alone? Why did they affect you so badly? Did they stop you doing something important?

Write down everything that the younger you was struggling with. All of it.

If you also have experience in a field other than coaching: What issue/gap have you detected (or can you find) that is a problem for some people in that field or industry? Why is it a problem? For whom in particular is it a problem? How does this problem manifest itself? What is the biggest pain-point for the individual that is affected by it?

Make your notes. Write as much as you can, even if it doesn't all make sense yet. In fact, it probably won't make proper sense yet, and that's ok.

Inventing a Person...

You are now going to create a fictitious person. Give this individual as much detail as you possibly can to make them into a real, believable person, who is based entirely on your thoughts and feelings about your ideal client. Trust me, creating this person is simply ***the most important bit of marketing activity you can do!***

You are going to describe this person in as much detail as I have described Stella. The object is to get to know them so that you can think and speak like her/him and know what they need to hear from you to think 'that's me!' when you talk to them in your marketing material. If you're tempted to write 'I don't know' in answer to any of the questions below, then think again. It's your job to know. If you need to do some research, then do it. I can't stress enough that this is the single most important piece of work you can do to generate paying clients; bar none.

Can They Afford You?

There is no point defining a client who can't afford to pay you, is there? I have spoken to so many coaches who want to coach the poor and disadvantaged, as a way of giving back to society. I understand the altruism, but there is something that you really need to understand, before you set off down this road.

Being worried about money isn't a great place for a coach to be. Having one's financial bases covered is a much healthier place to be. Define an ideal client who can afford you, and then, when you have a coaching practice full of paying clients, you can do all the altruistic coaching you want to do.

Overleaf are a whole load of questions to help you define your client. There's also a downloadable version of this ICA-creation document at thecoachingrevolution.com/book-downloads.

My Ideal Client Avatar

Name:

Age:

Gender:

Hair colour:

Eye colour:

Marital status:

Children (including names and ages):

Residence (what kind, where?):

Income:

Occupation:

Religion:

Lifestyle choices (eg vegan):

Favourite Books:

Favourite Magazines/newspapers/periodicals:
Favourite TV shows:

Favourite music:

Hobbies:

What do they Google?

What conferences to they attend?

What gigs do they attend?

What do they do in their free time?

What is/are their guilty pleasure(s)?

What's their favourite meal?

What kind of car do they drive?

Where do they go on holiday?

What's their favourite YouTube video?

The next two questions are critical:

1. What keeps them awake at night, worrying? (Be specific and remember that we are talking about a problem that you can help them with)
2. What do they fear the most? (Again, related to what you can help them with)

This is Hard!

I know that this is a tricky exercise. Persevere. It's worth it.

It is going to take you some time – a good couple of days of solid work, or a week or so of intermittent work.

Keep going until you have created a person who feels real to you. You must know them as well as I know Stella. Bear in mind that this is an exercise of both realistic and accurate information, and imagination. You are making this person up, but within set criteria. What I mean by this is that the various aspects of your ICAs life need to be believable.

Let me give you some examples of things that aren't believable:

If your ICA is a retail assistant, they're not going to have an income of £70k.

If they're the CEO of some massive organisation, they're not going to have hobbies that include sailing every Sunday, golfing twice a week, and camping with the family; they're too time poor to have all those hobbies.

If they're a millennial, you can't opt out of the question about YouTube by saying that they don't watch any videos, because they absolutely do!

If they've been out of work for 2 years and are claiming benefits, they are not going to be able to afford you. This is a very important point. You need to create an ICA who can actually afford to pay you!

If you find it difficult to answer some of the questions about your ICA, don't huff and puff or give up – research them!

Perfecting Your ICA

You will discover that you feel uncertain about whether or not you've done the ICA work correctly. That's normal. You'll also wonder if your ICA is good enough and/or complete. That's also normal.

The thing about your ICA is that you probably have to have several goes at them, to keep polishing and honing them, until they feel real. However, it's important to avoid the temptation is to polish so much that you never actually finish. It's important to finish your ICA to the point where you feel comfortable with the knowledge that you 'know' this person well enough to take some action and then make decisions on what to do next based on your results. Action, not perfection will save the day here.

Things to Remember

You need to think of either:

1. a client(s) you have really loved and who changed their lives for the better via coaching,
2. yourself when you found coaching,
3. those you know need coaching from your background and experience.

Then you need to think about what their big issue(s) are.

Cascading Issues

The 'awake at 3am' thing is crucially important. It's so important that everything else hinges on it. What you will find is that there is a single big issue from which every other issue cascades.

Let me explain using Stella.

Stella's 3am worry is that she can't get coaching clients. The things that cascade from that are:

- that she'll have to return to work for someone else
- that means that her children will be in before and after school care
- that also means she'll have to find childcare in the school holidays
- she'll be paying a stranger to bring up her precious children
- everyone who warned her this was a bad idea is right!
- how can she lift her head again in public?
- she feel's foolish for thinking she could do this!
- she'll feel like a failure – she **is** a failure
- who on earth did she think she was? People like her don't do things like this...

I could go on, but I suspect you've got the idea.

Your ICA will also have cascading problems and those cascades will make them feel unwell at night. They'll feel sweaty and sick with worry. You need to understand that cascade. In fact, it's vital that you do, because without that understanding, you won't get under their skin with your marketing message – which is coming later in this book.

Let's look at some other examples.

Examples

I'm going to use three different ICAs at various points in this book. They are, a new manager, a mum who wants her small business to succeed, and someone approaching retirement who is feeling anxious.

First of all, let's look at each in turn and see what worries they have cascading at 3am.

Our new manager lies awake worrying about his new job. These may be the cascading worries:

- am I up to this job?
- what if I'm not?
- worse still – what if someone else realises that I'm not!?
- my old friends will think I'm too big for my boots
- they'll stop wanting to hang out with me
- I won't have friends at work any more
- I don't know how to relate to my old teammates as their manager
- I'm scared of the difference that this new position will make

Our mum with her new small business may have similar worries to Stella:

- that the idea of having her own business demonstrates that she's too big for her boots
- that she **has** to make this business work, but it's not going to plan so far
- that if she can't she'll have to go back to working for someone else
- if she works for someone else, the flexibility she's looking for evaporates
- she'll have to find childcare in the school holidays
- people will think she's a failure because she couldn't make her business work
- she feels foolish for thinking she could be a business owner
- her mother told her this wouldn't work
- who on earth did she think she was? People like her don't do things like this...

Our retiree lies awake worrying about an uncertain, unstructured future. The cascading worries may be the following:

- I'm so OLD!
- I read that people die within a few years of retirement
- I'm going to miss my work colleagues dreadfully
- what will I do all day, every day without my routine?
- my spouse must be dreading my hanging around all day
- I don't have enough hobbies to fill my life
- my life is going to become pointless
- I'm going to lose my drive and ambition,
- my future is a grey fog in which all I can see is boredom

Your ICA

Your job is to sit and figure out what your ideal client is worrying about. What's keeping them awake at night? I've spoken to so many coaches who have blithely said 'I know who my ideal client is, it's a woman who's worried about the future' or some such vagary.

Can you see that knowing *exactly* who your ideal client is, and understanding *exactly* what's keeping them awake at night – that coaching will be able to resolve – means that you have a place to start that is meaningful when you start to talk to them?

The 'starting to talk to them' part of all this is your marketing message, and that's what we're going to look at next. You may find that you need to keep coming back to the ICA work when you start to craft your marketing message, because the ICA and the message are inextricably intertwined. The whole point of the ICA work is to make the next part of the job easier and to stop you being one of the countless coaches who talk about overcoming limiting beliefs etc.

They Will Change Over Time

The more you get to speak to people who fit your ICA profile, the more real your ICA will become. Stella has grown as a person (!!) over the last two years and I know her better now than I did when I started. I understand her frustration more than I did, which means that I can add to my marketing message (coming up in the next chapter).

What you need to remember is that this ICA is not necessarily forever, they are for now, but you need to give them a fair crack of the whip before you change them. What I mean is at least 6 months of focused effort directed towards your ICA. At that point, you will know them like a close friend. They will be with you most of the time and you will know what they need to hear to think *Gosh! They're talking about me!.*

I created Stella in September 2017. Initially, I intended to give her my utter focus for 6 months. She's still my ICA more than two years later and will remain so for as long as talking to her generates inbound enquiries for us, and business for The Coaching Revolution.

Please resist the urge to throw away what you've done and start again from scratch. Action rather than perfection is the aim of the game here (repeating myself I know, but this is important!). If Stella is still evolving after more than two years, don't throw in the towel on your ICA after two days!

Equally, please resist the urge to try to market to an ideal client for, say, eight weeks and then scrap everything, because you're not flooded with enquiries. Rather than throwing in the towel, work out why you're not getting enquiries, and tweak what you're doing. (More on this in a later chapter.)

Now that you have an understanding of what you're aiming for, may I suggest that you go back to the ICA questions that I set for you and see if any of your answers need updating? Remember that you absolutely **do** need to know things like job title and income level, because without these, you won't find your ICA in the real world. Don't roll your eyes and decide that this is nonsense, because I promise you, this works! Roll up your sleeves and do the work, your business will thank you for it.

A Mind Monkey Worthy Of Mention

One of the things that you will have heard, before you started reading this book – and you have probably heard it repeatedly – are those dreaded words *I can't afford it*.

I can promise you that those words are usually said when the person saying them doesn't recognise the value in what you are offering. When people do recognise the value, they can afford it.

When someone says "I can't afford it" they don't mean that literally. They don't mean *if I buy this, I'm going to ruin myself financially.* What they really mean is that they don't understand the value of what you're offering. We all do this. We say that we can't afford something if we can't see how it will help us to solve a problem we have or fulfil a need we have. We also do the opposite. We will move heaven and earth to afford something that we do see the value in.

The words *I can't afford it* really mean this; *you need to give me more information about what it is that you are offering. As it stands, I can't see how my life will be enhanced in any way by working with you.*

The response 'I can't afford it' often means:

- I'm not excited by what you say
- This doesn't sound like something that will help me to succeed

- I'm not convinced
- I don't trust you enough to give you money

The reason that people don't actually use those words is because in the main, people are nice. They don't want to hurt your feelings by saying what they're really thinking, and they know that no one is ever going to challenge *I can't afford it* so that's what they say.

Let me reassure you that by the time you've a) read and b) implemented everything in this book, you will rarely get the *I can't afford it* response.

Jenny Goody Case Study

Jenny is a dental practice manager, with many years' experience under her belt. Jenny wanted to create a consulting business primarily and was also very interested in what coaching could bring to her offering, and to her clients.

What follows is Jenny in her own words, from an interview we had together.

Tell Me About Jenny

Jenny said: I've been working as a practice manager for a number of years – too many years! – and I've got lots of experience in managing, but I've exhausted being a practice manager. I've done it and was getting bored. I wanted a new challenge and I thought, what is it that I can do? I'm a person that likes to help people; I like to help people reach their goals and to see them succeed. I hate to see people struggling.

I sat down and thought about what is it that I can already do? What do I have that would mean I don't have to learn a brand-new skill?

I'm currently working flexibly part-time, to sustain an income while I build my business. However, that's now got an end date.

How Jenny Found The Coaching Revolution

I Googled different ideas of what might be available to someone like me, who ultimately wants to be self-employed. I stumbled across coaching and I thought, actually this is something I could probably do. A mixture of coaching and consulting may be the answer to what I'm looking for, using all of the skills that I've got in the best way possible. I came across The Coaching Revolution and I read about what you offer to people like me, those without a coaching qualification, and I thought, you know what, this is really starting to tick boxes with me. I think this is something that is going to be the answer to what I want to do for my future. The combination of mentoring, business support, and an internationally recognised coaching qualification was perfect.

You and I had a couple of conversations and I thought *this is really exactly what I want*. The support that I need to achieve what I want is built in, because the biggest fear holding me back was doing something alone and failing.

That conversation with you, Sarah, was really reassuring. It made me confident that I could do exactly what I wanted to do and had the support of all of you mentors at The Coaching Revolution to make sure that I wasn't going to go off track. It made me confident that ultimately, I won't fail.

What Did You Want From The Coaching Revolution?

I really wanted to have a knowledge source that would be there for me to help me set up my business. Having never done it before I was worried about detail. I've run businesses, but they have never been my own business. I needed to know how to get those clients.

When you work as a manager, you think you know how to get clients. But that's sorted out for you when you work in a corporate, you just implement a prearranged marketing strategy. When there's a corporate name there, that's already known to your clients that's one thing. However, when you're setting out in business on your own, there's a whole wide world out there that I didn't know. I thought right, I know what I want to do, I've even got it down on paper. I also know who I want to talk to and be my client. **How** do I actually get those people to be my clients and get going on this? Ultimately, how do I swap my expertise, for their money!

That was the main thing I really was looking for in the Coaching Revolution, and I have to say, I have been guided through how to do that. I've created my ideal client; I know how to talk to them and (as my client is embedded within a corporation) how to make sure that I've got buy in at the right level. That's been one of the biggest things I've learned really. It seems so obvious when you sit and do the exercise with your mentor, but I would never have got there on my own, even with all my years of experience. I think I would have messed around the edges and hoped that I got there. But because The Coaching Revolution is so good at letting me focus on one thing at a time and teaching me how to do that thing, I've got there, and I've got my first clients.

How Did You Find The ICF Credential Course?

Absolutely brilliant! It's a really unique course. Online learning is something I've never done before; learning in that style on webinars is time-consuming. I'm a mum of two young children and employed as well, so I had to juggle things.

However, the actual skill is just so eye opening. It is really enriching in terms of giving you new ways of working and the confidence that I really needed. To be honest, it gave me a whole new outlook on coaching. I thought I knew what coaching was, and it turns out that I didn't! I had a specific way of working, which, it turns out was mentoring. Having true coaching to add to the mentoring tools I use with my clients has been amazing.

My fellow students and I are still supportive of one another now and it's been the making of my journey to becoming a coach.

How Have You Found Working With The Coaching Revolution?

What I've been doing with The Coaching Revolution has fitted in with being a mum and working part-time. This whole thing has just developed at a really natural pace. I'm not under any pressure to proceed any faster than is comfortable. Paul Snell, my Coaching Revolution mentor is very supportive of that. He never says, "you've not done this by that date Jenny, what's going on?" It's my journey, I'm in control. He is there when I need him and is always available to help me move on to the next step. Everything's working very well, I'm really pleased with what The Coaching Revolution and I are doing together.

My time is shared between organising two children, my employed work and setting up my business. When I get any spare time, it all goes into my business. Honestly, if I was a different person joining The Coaching Revolution, if I didn't have young children, and wasn't in my shoes, I'd probably be further on than I am, because I'd have 24 hours a day to dedicate to business-building. But I'm not that person, I'm very time poor. However, I am very determined and I'm already making it work. I know that you and all of The Coaching Revolution community are behind me 100% of the way to ensure I succeed.

What Was Unexpected About Working With Us?

I have discovered that being self-employed isn't it as lonely as I first thought it was going to be. I thought I would be sitting at home, with my laptop, coaching a few people here and there. I thought that not having a network of colleagues around me and going out to work every day would be a really hard thing for me. I am a very people person and I was worried I'd be lonely.

However, the thing that I've discovered is, by being with The Coaching Revolution, I have oodles of network support and community. I've made friendships with my cohort from the ICF accreditation course, as well as the rest of the community. All the mentees and the mentors within the Coaching Revolution are available in the private Facebook group, or pick up the phone, or drop someone an email and bingo! There's somebody there to help you answer a question. Whether you need help all the time (in the beginning mainly) or just a little bit, there's always someone there. We have our virtual network, but best of all, when we have our quarterly meetings, we actually get to see each other for real.

I'm not alone and that just feels good. I now know that I don't have to be in a workplace with colleagues around me. I'm my home and I still have colleagues around me albeit in a very different way. That's been the most unexpected, and fantastic discovery for me.

What Was The Most Challenging Thing?

I think the most challenging thing for me was just getting off the starting blocks. I'm still working at gaining momentum. It's a very self-disciplined thing to have to do, I have to push myself all the time to stay focused and get things done.

I've already mentioned my time limitations, which of course is a challenge too. I have to be really organised and have everything in the right place so that when I do have time, I can work productively. I think that still hangs over me now because I'm not quite there with everything, I'm still developing my website and I'm still writing my materials.

However, I am supported in those challenges. I just have to email Paul and say 'I'm not sure about wording for a contract' for example and he'll tell me to send it to him, he'll look it over and we'll sort it out quickly and without fuss. What that means is that challenge is no longer a challenge; it's been resolved, and can I move on to the next thing. So challenges do exist, but I'm not alone. Without doubt, that's the most important thing for me; I've got a resource to turn to and get the help that I need, when I need it.

How Do You Feel About The Future?

I am so excited!

Right now, I've got so much in the pipeline. I feel like I have a little ball of fire inside me that's just about to go *poof* any moment, once everything falls into place. I've had a meeting with a connection who's going to work alongside me in terms of networking and sharing materials. I'm coaching a client – which is just so exciting – and she's really getting so much out of it that she's already shouting about me and about how good my coaching has been for her, which is really, really excellent. I'm doing some life coaching with another client and she is just embracing everything that we're doing together.

I've got another meeting coming up with another colleague who is in the same arena as me and we're going to discuss how we could be referral partners.

I feel a nervous anticipation – in a good way – of what's around the corner. I'd love to be able to see what the future looks like already. I'm so happy that I've got all my pipeline of enquiries already flowing. I think it can only grow and grow and the secret is starting with small steps. I'm working on getting some great testimonials, and I'm working on growing an excellent reputation. I can utilise and build on that on social media and on my website. That will springboard me into a whole new place of going totally self-employed, alone, which is my goal. I want to stop the part-time job. So yeah, I feel a fire of excitement inside!

What Advice Would You Give To Those Who Are Thinking Of Working With Us?

I would say that, take a few minutes and write down what it is that's really bugging you at the moment about having your own business, about where you are and who you are within that potential business.

Do a mind map of it and then identify those things that are most important to you. Once you've identified that, don't hold back on picking up that phone and having that conversation with The Coaching Revolution. You'll probably talk to Sarah, and she'll likely be able to provide you with the answers that you need and give you the reassurance that you can achieve what you want to in business. You can make it a really successful thing, you can get clients and you can become as happy as I am as a self-employed person, as a coach.

Don't hold back, just get in touch with them. You won't be sorry.

Talking to Your Ideal Client

Now that you've created your ICA, you can begin to think about what your ICA needs to hear, to understand why they should want to work with you. In this chapter we're going to look at how to create your marketing message and why you're doing it.

Every coach's ICA will be different and using The Coaching Revolution's way of marketing will mean that your marketing message is unique. It isn't a cookie-cutter presentation that countless other coaches have and are delivering, it's yours. No one else will be out there delivering your marketing message to the type of client that you in particular want to work with, the one who is personified in your ICA.

The Coaching Industry Is NOT Saturated

Let me expand on the fact that every coach's ICA will be different. and explain to you why this way of marketing your coaching business will mean that you never operate in a saturated market.

Thinking about every mentee that The Coaching Revolution has ever had, no two have the same ideal client. In fact, I could go as far as saying that it's really hard to have the same

ICA as someone else. After all, considering the amount of work you've put in to creating your ICA, you know that they are 'real'. What this means is that just as we are all different, so are our ICAs.

I regularly speak to coaches who say that there are, for example, three other coaches in their town all competing for the same business. Using our method of marketing your coaching business means the real-life outcome is that we could all live *in the same street* and we wouldn't be in competition with one another. This is why an ideal client is so much more valuable than a niche. A niche might be small businesses and if that's the niche of half a dozen coaches in a single town they would all be fighting for the same clients.

You may have seen a real-life example of this in action. If you have ever been to a business networking event that is specifically aimed at small business owners, it's not unusual for there to be a few coaches there, all sniffing around for the same business. In their introduction, they'll say that they work with small business owners to help them reach their business goals and to overcome their limiting business beliefs (sound familiar?) to make more profit. By the time you get to the fifth or sixth coach, they're all saying the same thing.

A coach who uses our marketing methods would never say anything so generic. If one of our coaches has an ICA who's a small business owner, they would describe **exactly** the specific sort of small business owner that they work with and they would articulate exactly what that kind of business owner is struggling with. The effect is that some of the people in the room will prick up their ears. They will think, *gosh, that person works with people like me!* And that's what you're looking for. Not everyone in the room will fit your ideal client profile and that's ok. However, providing you've done the work, the reason you're even at this particular networking event is because you know that people who fit your ideal client profile are likely to be there too. The coach who attends as many networking events as possible, thinking that everyone there is a potential client is doomed to disappointment. The coach who attends carefully chosen events, based on where they know their ideal client is, will pick up paying clients.

Why You Need A Marketing Message

The basic function of your marketing message is to create trust and engender a feeling of confidence in what you do in your potential clients. If you can do this, you will generate inbound enquiries. I can't tell you how wonderful it feels when the first inbound enquiry lands in your inbox. I still get a thrill of delight when someone who has seen what I've written, recognises themselves in what I wrote and wants to talk to me because of it.

Create Trust

In his book *The Speed of Trust*, Stephen Covey says that the basic foundations of trust are threefold. They are integrity, intent and behaviour. Let's look at each of these in a nutshell, in respect of your coaching business.

- Integrity is being honest about who you are and what you do.
- Intent is your motive for doing what you do.
- Behaviour is how you demonstrate the previous two.

Integrity

Coaches are usually 'people-people'. They have big hearts and they want to coach because they believe in it as a process for improving people's lives. To go back to what I said at the beginning, coaches know that coaching is a superpower.

You don't want to copy someone else; you want to be you. The best thing about being you is that you are the very best at it. No one else can come close to being as good as you are at being you.

I know that this may seem like I'm stating the obvious; but be truthful. Lying about what you can do for people and how you can do it, may get a rush of interest at the beginning, but it does nothing for your integrity.

I had the misfortune to be involved with a company who said one thing and did another. The amount of micromanaging and the number of overbearing 'compliance' rules should perhaps have alerted me to their underhand practices. However, I utterly believed their marketing message. The horrible sense of disappointment and disgust that I felt when I found out the true picture was overwhelming. You really don't want people feeling this about your coaching business and your brand.

Intent

We coaches are people-people as I have said repeatedly. It's important that your intention is clear in your messaging. Your intention is to support your client to become the very best that they can be – it's that simple.

Make sure that your intention is clear for all to see. Keep it focused on your client and not on you. Those coaches who are simply in it for the money are easy to spot once you actually listen to them.

Behaviour

When you show up, wherever you show up, your behaviour will demonstrate your integrity and your intent.

It's often remarked upon that I'm very passionate about what I do. My behaviour demonstrates my commitment to our mission. Our mission is based upon our collective integrity and our intention.

The reason I seem passionate about what we do is because I want to change the world. Specifically, I want to change the world via coaching and I can't do that on my own. So, dear coach, you are the focus of my behaviour. You and others like you, along with the knowledge and skills I can teach you, can change the world. My part in that is to make sure that you know how to get clients to actually begin the change.

Marketing Isn't About YOU!

What most coaches fail to do when they talk about their work, is make it relevant to their potential clients.

If you ask a coach what they do, they try to define coaching and they'll talk about themselves. They may tell you – in detail – what a coaching session entails, and how they'll help you to set goals, break them down into milestones and then support you to overcome mental barriers, or limiting beliefs (I know I sound like a stuck record, but so do the hundreds and hundreds of coaches I have heard use these phrases!). They can talk about the process of coaching happily, for hours.

Next, they may tell you all about their qualifications and experience. They'll indulge in a bit of humble bragging about how fabulous their particular qualification is.

The sad fact is that nobody cares! Actually, that's not fair; the coach cares, the client doesn't.

Coaches are constantly astonished that the person they're talking to doesn't get excited about what they're saying. They're slightly offended that their gleaming resumé doesn't seem to inspire awe in the person they're talking to. Coaches don't seem to realise that marketing their coaching business doesn't involve talking about either the process of coaching, or themselves.

Coaching qualifications are irrelevant to clients. Okay, they may be more relevant if you want to work on an employed basis in a corporate setting, but when you're running your own coaching business, it's rare that people actually ask (or are even interested in) your qualification.

Here's a fact; the only people who have ever asked me about my coaching qualifications are other coaches. I can be even more specific than that actually, they are usually other coaches who have looked at me in annoyance because I've been making a living at this for a long time and they're struggling to find paying clients. They can't understand how their gold-plated qualifications haven't resulted in the clients that they expected, nor how I seem to find clients so easily. Please understand that I'm absolutely not saying that your coaching qualification is irrelevant. It's not. However, it is irrelevant in terms of *marketing* your coaching business.

Here's another fact; people do not buy processes or qualifications. They buy results.

What Results Can Your Client Expect?

If, as I suspect, you're still a little confused about (if not downright reluctant to accept) the ideal client concept, then your answer to the question 'what results can your clients expect?' will always be 'it depends'. It depends on the individual, it depends on their situation, it depends on their willingness to embrace change, it depends on so many variables.

The problem with that answer is that it's impossible to create a marketing message from it.

If you let go of your reluctance and embrace the ideal client concept, suddenly, your marketing message becomes clear. Let's go back to our examples:

New Managers – if you coach managers in the first few months of their new role, then the results that they can reasonably expect include:

- Their new role becomes more comfortable
- They are managing their teams better

- They are not overwhelmed
- They're enjoying the work
- They have a better understanding of how the new role differs from their old 'delivery' role
- They're no longer lying awake at 3am feeling anxious and worried that they're going to lose their old friends or that they're not good enough

Mumpreneurs – if you want to coach mums who have started businesses in order to be able to stay at home with their children, then the results they can reasonably expect include:

- They take action and get stuff done
- They actually get customers (rather than focusing on other aspects of their businesses)
- They manage their time more effectively
- They don't feel overwhelmed
- They have a financial goal, which they are working towards
- They're not lying awake at 3am worrying that their business isn't making money, which means that they have to go back into employment and pay someone else to bring up their children

Retirees – if you want to coach those who are approaching retirement, perhaps with some trepidation, the results that they can reasonably expect include:

- They feel less anxious about leaving the workplace
- Their partner will also feel more confident
- They will have a plan of action
- They actually take that action
- They feel fulfilled, rather than lost

- They're not lying awake at 3am worrying about losing the framework of their whole life, which to date has been their job.

Do you get the idea? If any of those people, the new manager, the mumpreneur or the retiree were to read their particular list of outcomes, they'd think *s/he's talking about me, those are the outcomes I want!* and that is exactly what you're looking for.

Self-Selecting Clients

What a coach needs, is a way of generating interest in their work which makes clients come to them. It's sometimes called 'attraction marketing' (and not to be confused with the Law of Attraction, which is not a business development tool at all).

In a perfect world, the one you are going to create for your business, clients will hear or read what you say in your marketing and think 'this coach is talking about me!'. The next step for that individual will be to ask for more information. This is what The Coaching Revolution is all about; creating situations in which your client comes to you. Another way of describing this is 'generating inbound enquiries'.

Now that you've created your ICA from the work you did in the last few chapters, (you did do that work, right?) your next step is to create a marketing message that is directly aimed at them. Specifically, you going to talk about the problems that they have, and the outcomes that they can expect from working with you.

Talking About Negatives

Before we get creating your marketing toolkit, there is a mind monkey that we need to deal with. Coaches are very positive, forward-thinking and optimistic people. It's why coaching suits us, we're all about the positive future. However, in your marketing message, you are going to talk about problems that your ICA has. This messes with the heads of many coaches. Coaches don't want to talk about problems, they want to talk about *overcoming* problems.

I cannot stress enough, how much you need to let go of this limiting belief. That's what this is, plainly and simply, it's a limiting belief. Hanging on to this belief can cost you your coaching business. The 82% (most of them anyway) almost certainly held on to this particular mind monkey and it cost them dearly.

I know I've already said this, but I'm going to say it again. This book and our process isn't about your actual coaching delivery. Coaches can get really hung up about the fact that a coach can coach anyone, and that coaching is specifically **not** about the coach's skills and knowledge. Please can I reassure you that you are not going to insert your skills and knowledge into a coaching session, but it's absolutely vital that you insert them into your marketing message, otherwise your message will be far too vague for anyone to understand the benefit to them of working with you.

Why Do People Buy?

People buy for one of two reasons; to solve a problem or to

fulfil a need. Every purchase we make fits one of these two categories. Let me give you a couple of examples:

A car – we buy a car to solve the problem of getting around, and maybe to fulfil a need to be able to travel more widely and/or more quickly than public transport. However, we might choose to buy the top-of-the-range Mercedes in particular to fulfil a personal need; the need to make a statement about where we feel that we fit in the social hierarchy.

A laptop – we buy a laptop to maybe solve the problems of both accessing the internet from home and keeping up with routine family-based administration. We may buy an Apple laptop in particular, to fulfil a perceived aesthetic or functionality need.

Those aren't perfect examples, nor are they necessarily accurate problems or needs for everyone. However, they do explain what I'm trying to get across.

What this problem/need thing means to you, is that your marketing needs to address a specific problem or need that your ICA has and offer a solution to that problem or need. It has to address this so well that your message is the glove that fits the hand of their problem or need. In crafting some portions of your message, you need to let go of the 'eternal optimist' within you and accept that you're going to have to talk about issues that your ICA has, that they want to get rid of.

It's a chunky piece of work, so let's get going.

Your Marketing Toolkit

At The Coaching Revolution, we refer to the process I'm about to take you through as creating your marketing toolkit. By the end of the exercise, you'll have 40 minutes' worth of material that you can, if you wish, stand up and deliver to audiences as a keynote presentation. However, may I say here and now, that you **don't have to deliver it as a presentation if you don't want to**. Please don't get hung up on whether or not you want to do public speaking. That's a whole other book (one that I currently have no plans to write) and you can use the message you're going to create in myriad different ways without ever, *ever* delivering as a speaker.

If on the other hand you're like me and love public speaking, you're going to end up with a talk that's so focused and punchy, that if you deliver it in the right places (those places being exactly where your ICA is), then it will bring you those inbound enquiries, simple as that.

The toolkit you'll end up with in crafting this marketing message in the format we prescribe, is your *complete* toolkit for attracting clients. What I mean by this is that you will have enough marketing material in this toolkit to use it to create articles or blog posts, short and long-form social media content, videos, podcasts... You get the idea? You will be able to create lots of different content from the toolkit that you create.

A Chunky Piece of Work

Be aware before you start this process that it's a big piece of work. I can also tell you that your first, second and possibly even third iterations of it won't be good enough. You need to keep going to hone it and hone it, until you're left with a shining jewel of a thing.

The main mistakes that coaches make here is that they're far too wordy. Worse still, they talk in coach-speak and not client-speak. A combination of a) being too wordy and b) coach-speak makes your marketing unintelligible to your potential client, which negates all your hard work.

Top Tips Before You Start

- Make sure – doubly sure – that you're speaking in client-speak and not coach-speak. What I mean by that is check every single word for jargon. If it's jargon, remove it. Forget at your peril that coaches' language is not your client's language.

- Be clear in what you say. Don't use 50 words if 10 can convey your message. Equally, don't use fancy language. Without exception simplicity and clarity win the day. The more complex your language, the easier it is for it to be misinterpreted. Conversely, the fewer words you use, and the more simple your language, the easier it is for your potential client to understand what you're offering and therefore want to engage with you. A top tip I was given by a mentor of mine was edit like you're being paid £1000 for every word you remove. Fewer good words are better than many 'woolly' ones.

- Don't confuse. Confused people zone out. They simply stop listening. What they never, ever do is buy from you.

> Know this; the coach with the clearest message will get the client – even if they're not the best coach.

Let me just elaborate on that last point for a moment. It doesn't actually matter whether you're the best coach in the world. If you don't get any clients to coach, it's actually irrelevant, isn't it?

Without exception, the coaches with the best businesses are those who know exactly who their clients are, and deliver a simple, clear and compelling message to them. The message says this; I understand you have a problem; I know that this problem is impacting your life in unacceptable ways, these are those ways. and I know how to help you overcome this problem.

What we're going to do in the next chapter is create your simple, clear, concise marketing message. There's a downloadable PDF to help you with this available at thecoachingrevolution.com/book-downloads.

Creating Your Toolkit

Here are eight headings, you need enough in each to make five minutes of a spoken presentation (roughly!). Again, please don't get hung up on the spoken bit, it's just a good way of measuring length. If you never, ever stand up on your back legs to present this as a talk, that's ok. All the introverts reading this can breathe easy; no one is going to make you do public speaking, unless you want to that is.

1 – Introduce yourself

The purpose of this section is to very quickly establish yourself as someone worthy of listing to. That doesn't mean that you drone on and on about your qualifications and give a month by month account of your 30-year career.

This bit of your presentation is the one part that is about you. This is the shortest section. The reason for this is that, at this point, no one cares about you. They only care about what you can do for them. However, it's rude not to introduce yourself, so do so briefly.

Remembering what we discussed earlier about behaviour, intent and integrity, you're going to introduce yourself. Let me reiterate, because it's important, be brief.

Your introduction doesn't need to contain anything about the highly commended certificate you earned for swimming in secondary school. It almost certainly doesn't want to be a rendition of your CV either. The caveat to this is that if, like one of our mentees, you've been a hostage negotiator and you were responsible for clearing the minefield that Princess Diana subsequently strolled through, you may want to mention that. This guy's CV is exceptional, fascinating, and worthy of mention. Most people's aren't.

Your coaching qualification isn't important here. No one will know what it means anyway, will they? ICF PCC? Lovely, what does that mean? Remember, the only people really interested in your qualifications are other coaches, so skip it.

However, it's important to establish yourself as an expert in the topic you're going to talk about, so mention relevant history. My version of this section talks about the fact that my career has spanned 30+ years, and other than 7 years out for child-rearing, and about 3 working as an employee, the rest has been self-employed. I talk about the fact that when I was a single mum, every bean that came into my house was earned by me via my coaching business, and that both of my children, two dogs and three cats are still alive to tell the tale; no one starved! In short, you can trust me when I talk about building a coaching business. I've been there, and I've done it.

2 – Overview

The purpose of this section is twofold, one it's to move the conversation away from you and onto your ICA and two, it's to engage their curiosity.

This section is best written last, because this is the part where you give a brief overview of what your presentation is about. Rather like the introduction to an essay, you will only be able to complete this section once you have clarity about where your message is taking you.

However, just so you know when you get to this bit, what you need to do here is tell them what you're going to tell them. The best and most memorable messages follow this framework:

- Tell them what you're going to tell them
- Tell them
- Tell them what you told them

The overview is the first of these three things.

My overview section talks about the fact that I'm going to describe the journey of the vast majority of coaches, from discovering coaching, through gaining a qualification and onto extreme frustration because they can't find clients. I tell my audience that I'm going to explain why they can't find clients and that it's not their fault, and I'm going to outline a simple process that will help them to change their client-free situation, to one that contains as many clients as they can handle.

3 – Fact or question

The purpose of this section is to get your audience to prick up their ears. You need to hit the nail on the head with this in a way that makes your ICA think *Wow! S/he's talking about ME!*

State a tantalising or controversial fact about the topic you're going to present. For example, the fact I use (endlessly!) is that there is a global statistic that says that 82% of coaching businesses will fail in the first two years. This fact is shocking and almost unbelievable. The fact it comes from the ICF gives it both the credibility and gravitas to make my ICA sit up and take notice.

What does your ICA need to hear that will make them sit up and listen (or stop scrolling and read)?

To go back to our new managers, mumpreneurs and retiree ICAs mentioned earlier, here are some examples of the kind of thing you want to look for:

New managers – A Gallup poll of over a million people showed that 75% of people who left a role voluntarily, did so because of their manager and not because of the job itself.

Mumpreneurs – In 2018, there were 5.7 million private sector businesses in the UK. 75% of these were people working in a one-person business.

Retiree – Dr Shigeaki Hinohara, a Japanese doctor and longevity expert, says that not retiring at all is the key to a long life.

Can you see how you can go on to build from these challenging statements to craft an interesting message?

Bulk out your statement. Remember, you're looking for 5 minutes of content if you read it out loud. My 82% statement is followed by me explaining that actually the part that says 'in the first two years' is, in my experience, a red herring. Actually it's not that 82% of coaches create coaching businesses that thrive, and then somehow trip up before they reach their second anniversary. The truth is that the vast majority of that 82% fail to launch in the first place.

4 – Expansion

This is the part of your message where you go on to expand upon the theme you set in your challenging statement or question.

For example, if your ICA is the new manager, you could go on to talk about how not to be that 'idiot boss' that makes people leave. For the mumpreneur you can talk about either the fact that she is not alone in her quest to generate her income under her own steam. The retiree wants to hear how they can be the person to buck the trend of this statistic. (Just for the record, it seems to be that keeping active and intellectually stimulated was key.)

The content of this section is intended for you to demonstrate your knowledge and understanding of your ICA and this particular aspect of their life. Specifically, that this particular aspect of their lives is a right royal pain in the rear to them and is impacting on their ability to sleep well at night. Please remember, this isn't about your coaching skills. This is about you helping someone to understand, by using relevant and real-life examples, how coaching can transform their lives.

This section is where you'll struggle if you've not actually completed the ICA work from the last chapter. If you have defined the problem your ICA is facing, you'll have a significant understanding of that problem and you'll be able to articulate exactly how the problem is manifesting in the life of your ICA. If you didn't do the work, well honestly, you're going to struggle, so go back to the last chapter and do the work! (I know I keep saying this, and I'm going to continue to nag. Save yourself the pang of guilt when you read it and just do the work!)

This is the section where you talk about negative behaviours and/or thoughts that your ICA will have experienced in the particular situation you're discussing. You want to have clarity when you talk about this, because this is the part of the KNP where your understanding and empathy need to be at their greatest. You're effectively saying *You do/think this, and you wish you didn't, but you don't seem to be able to get out of the pattern of behaviour/thoughts.* Your ICA should be metaphorically (or literally) sitting up and really becoming engaged as they hear you describe *exactly* the behaviour they are struggling with.

Let me give you some examples:

New manager – people in this position are people who are very good at the job they were doing before their promotion. Previously, they were only responsible for themselves and for their work and they were completely confident in that position. Now, they are beset with doubts about whether or not they can do the job they have. They've read Laurence J. Peter's book *The Peter Principle* and are worried that they're going to be incompetent.

This ICA doesn't want to come across as the idiot manager

(that person we've all experienced who was a complete and utter nightmare to work for) but equally, they want their team to respect them and they don't want to be a pushover. There is a fine line between being a great manager and a nightmare, and this ICA really, *really* wants to get it right. However, very few of us get training for this role. The fact that this ICA was good at what they did means that there's an expectation that they'll be good managing a team and this is causing this ICA sleepless nights. If only they could get a handle on what the differences actually **are** in the two roles, rather than how those differences **feel**, which is pretty grim. This person just knows that if only they could get into the swing of this new role, without losing friends, it will then be ok.

Mumpreneur – this woman had a job in which she thrived before she had children. It was absolutely her intention to give birth and go back to work happily at the end of her maternity leave. However, no one prepared her for the massive shift in priorities and values that comes with having a baby and now, she doesn't want to go back to work. She still needs to bring in some money and so she's decided to start her own business. It turns out that she's not as good at the 'getting customers' part of the business as she thought she was going to be. She was sure that if her product/service was right, that the customers would just come and that's not proved to be the case. If she doesn't make this work, she's going to have to go back to work, which is crazy, because by the time she factors in the childcare and the cost of the commute, she will be earning a fraction of what she did before. She only needs to make a few hundred pounds a month for this to be perfect, and yet those customers seem so illusive. If only she could crack the customer part of her business and her reluctance to get out there and find them, she knows that she can make this work.

Retiree – this ICA has spent their whole lives with the framework and routine of employment. They have always talked about what they're going to do when they retire, and they've got their ducks in a row financially. However, with the date of retirement looming, there's a feeling of dread that they just can't seem to shake, and they are not looking forward to it. They know, intellectually that they should be optimistic about the future, and so they are worried about saying out loud that they're dreading it. If only they had a framework for retirement that could help them to feel secure.

Can you see how these three types of ICA would be able to hear their own thoughts in what I've described? That's what you need to do for your ICA.

My content for this section talks about the anxiety my ICA has around what getting clients actually entails. That in their mind, there is something that says that if their coaching was good enough, the clients would come. Logically, they know that's not true, but it *feels* that way. The fact that the few people they have coached have raved about them strikes a dissonant chord in their head – how can they possibly be good at coaching if they can't find clients via strategy sessions? Their partner is beginning to wonder out loud how long this is going to continue, without them earning a single penny, and honestly, it's keeping them awake at night. They know that coaching businesses exist, why can't they make theirs work?

5 – Explanation

In this section of your marketing message, you're going to

explain to your ICA the reason why the behaviour and/or negative thought patterns you've just described exists.

The purpose of this section is to reassure your ICA that firstly, they're not alone and that what they're experiencing is both normal and frequently occurring. It is also to help them see why they have got themselves into this particular funk and can't see their way out. It is to provide clarity about the path to being able to stop worrying, start doing something proactive and therefore sleep better.

The last sentence for each of the descriptions in part 4, is the part you're going to expand on here. Let me give you some examples:

New manager – *If only they could get into the swing of this new role, without losing friends, they feel sure it will then be ok.*

This ICA needs to hear that it is perfectly natural for new managers to wonder if they're up to the job. They also need to hear that having someone to talk to about their hopes and dreams, as well as their fears and worries can help them to achieve and overcome them respectively. You're inserting the idea into their brains that maybe an outside person (you!) can help them, because they are not as useless, or uniquely incapable as they believe.

Mumpreneur – *If only she could crack the customer part of her business, she knows that she can make this work.*

This ICA needs to understand that finding customers isn't impossible. She also needs to understand that she isn't alone, that her anxieties are shared by all new mums who decide to start a business. She needs to know that someone actually believes that she can do this. She needs the idea that having someone to bounce ideas off, and to sound things out with (you!) inserting into her thought process.

Retiree – *If only s/he had a framework for retirement that could help them to feel secure.*

This ICA needs to understand that what they're feeling is completely normal, that it's quite common for people to feel anxious about such a massive change in their lives. It may be that this ICA doesn't realise that it's the structure and routine that they're grieving for. They need to understand that having someone to bounce ideas off, to share their fears and anxieties with without fear of judgment (you!) is a great idea. They need to understand that actually, retirement can be the most liberating part of their lives, allowing them to finally create their own structure, and routines that are perfect for them.

Do you see how this message is now becoming a story about your ICA? You are effectively describing your ICA, their ambitions and anxieties, in such a way that they are going to recognise themselves and feel relieved. Relieved because there is a real solution to a problem that they believed was entirely unique.

My content for this section talks about the fact that The Coaching Revolution has a plethora of coaches who are succeeding in building their coaching businesses. I talk about the fact that counter-intuitively, laser-focusing one's marketing efforts is much more effective than casting the net wide. I go on to talk about why they may feel resistance to this. I gently insert into their minds the idea that working 1:1 with someone who has already achieved the goal of a financially viable coaching business can turn their business around. Doing the work in a supported way can give them the business that they yearn for.

6 – Alternative

Here, you're going to offer a practical alternative to the anxiety and worrying that your ICA has been doing so far. It really helps if what you talk about seems like common sense.

This is the section of your marketing message where you're going to talk about the kind of results that your ICA can expect from working with you. Rather than making this about you (I can help you X, Y and Z) you're going to talk about what your ICA can expect to **feel** when they've resolved their issues. You are also going to leave them with a suggestion or two that they can walk away and immediately put into practice to alleviate some of their issues. Let me give you some examples:

New manager – this ICA needs to understand that being someone's manager and someone's friend are two different things, and that's ok. Sitting down with the friend whom you now manage to talk about the difference between those two roles really helps.

Mumpreneur – this ICA perhaps gets uncomfortable at the thought of selling. Specifically, she may be avoiding the sales part, and focusing too much on the other activities that make up her business. She needs a wake-up call and it's this: without customers, she doesn't have a business. She may also need to understand that selling doesn't have to be grubby or uncomfortable, that it's simply an extension of good customer service. Maybe she can write down her customer's journey, from unaware of the product/service, to happy customer? That way, she can see that the actual selling part isn't a thing on it's own, but part of a bigger customer service picture.

Retiree – this ICA needs to understand that it is possible to have a retirement that they can both look forward to and enjoy. They also need to understand that, first of all voicing their fears, and then having a plan for retirement can help to alleviate those feelings of anxiety. Even better, why not include his/her partner in crafting those plans in order to have something that both can really look forward to.

This section of your marketing message is about reassurance and your credibility. The thing about common sense is that it isn't actually very common. Your being able to talk both knowledgeably and reassuringly about something that is quite literally keeping your ICA awake at night will bring enormous comfort to those who fit your ICA profile. Don't forget, that fit doesn't have to be a bullseye, it can be anywhere on the dart board. If you directly address the thing that's keeping your ICA awake at night, you will always get kudos and therefore credibility.

Remember to include a 'give-away' in this section: A concrete suggestion of action that someone listening (or reading) can immediately take away and do, that will help them to get unstuck, or begin to get unstuck.

My giveaway is to suggest that the coach goes to Facebook and search for Coaching Republic, it's our free community for coaches who are building their businesses. It's full of workshops and master classes for them to enjoy. Your giveaway doesn't have to be a physical thing, nor does it have to be an invitation like mine. It simply needs to be an action that your ICA can put into action immediately, that will alleviate some of their anxiety and/or problem.

7 – Not Default Behaviour

This section is specifically here to reassure your ICA that their current behaviour, thoughts and feelings, are normal. The alternatives you suggested might sound like common sense, but common sense is rarely common. Your ICA needs to understand that you're not patronising them. You're not saying; *gosh how foolish are you, worrying about X, Y or Z! I know much better than you do about how you feel!*

What you're saying is this; *your thoughts and feelings are not unique, and they don't make you foolish. What you're feeling is completely normal for someone in your position. However, there are solutions to the issue that's giving you sleepless nights and I may be able to help you with those solutions.*

Let me give you some examples:

New manager – this ICA needs to understand that if their situation was unique, leadership training wouldn't exist, and yet it does and it's a big industry. Even if the company they're working for doesn't offer leadership training, that doesn't mean that they won't benefit from it. Specifically, having someone (a coach!) with whom they can talk and let off steam will not only help them sleep at night, it will also help them to succeed faster and better than they could alone.

Mumpreneur – this ICA needs to understand that she is not alone in her fears. She needs to understand that there are mothers everywhere who have had exactly the same 'I'll start a business' lightbulb moment as a solution to wanting to stay at home with their children. She also needs to understand that building a successful business (whatever her definition of success is) is possible. It mostly depends on her having someone to talk to (a coach!) who can help her see where she's getting in her own way, where her thoughts and feelings are a hindrance rather than a help.

Retiree – this ICA needs to understand that what they're feeling is very common; they're not ungrateful or foolish for feeling worried. S/he also needs to know that s/he doesn't have to navigate this massive life change alone. If s/he had someone to talk to and bounce ideas, hopes and fears off (a coach!) then creating a framework for a happy retirement will be a reality, not just hopeful.

Can you see what you're doing here? You are being very reassuring and comforting. You're supporting your ICA in their journey to understanding that they're not inadequate, or unique; they are simply suffering from what any normal person in their situation suffers from. What's more, you're reassuring them that they don't have to suffer!

My content for this section talks about the fact that my ICA isn't dumb for not knowing how to generate paying clients. We live in a world where our entire education systems are designed to create employees, not entrepreneurs. There is no reason whatsoever that my ICA should have the first clue about generating business. The fact that they don't is exactly why they grasped the idea of delivering strategy sessions so hard. It *feels* logical, it seems like it's the right thing to do. The fact that they're listening to me now means that it absolutely hasn't worked for them.

Don't brush this section aside, it's important.

8 – Encouragement

This section is all about encouragement. You are going to encourage your ICA to do something positive that will help them move forward from where they are now, to actually sleeping at night. You are going to strongly encourage them to take the action you have outlined in part 6 of your marketing message. You're going to tell them that knowing there are things they can do to help themselves, and actually doing those things are two different things.

Let me give you some examples:

New manager – perhaps you can suggest to this ICA that when they walk away (or stop reading), that they can immediately schedule a conversation with each of their team members. Encourage them to make that conversation two-way, and not simply a conversation in which they tell their team member what's what. You can talk about the respect that such a conversation will bring them, you can talk about them being able to move forward from being the *new* manager, to simply being the manager.

Mumpreneur – perhaps you can suggest that this ICA creates her own ICA? That she sits down to work out where she is most likely to gain paying customers? Help her to understand (just as you now do) that trying to sell her product/service to 'anyone who…' simply doesn't work.

Retiree – perhaps you could suggest to this ICA that there are a couple of things that they can do immediately that will help allay their fears. One is an acceptance of reality; the date of retirement will arrive whether they are anxious about it or looking forward to it. Accepting reality is an enormous step towards relief from fear. The other thing is to talk about their worries, perhaps with their partner. Once said out loud, fears are diminished.

My content in this part is to talk about the resources that are available for free in Coaching Republic to help them nail their own ICA. They can take enormous steps towards building their business by simply following the advice of The Coaching Revolution in Coaching Republic.

The overriding message that you need to give to your ICA here is that action removes fear. In suggesting possible actions, you again increase your credibility.

9 – Recap

Do you remember in section 2, the overview, we said you were going to tell them what you are going to tell them, then tell them, then tell them what you told them? Well this is the final part of that trinity. In the recap, you're going to briefly go over what you've said, just to refresh people's minds and remind them that there is a way out of the situation that they've found themselves in.

Let me give you some examples:

New manager – your recap might be; we've established that poor managers can have a massive impact on companies, after all, 75% of those who leave a job voluntarily do so because of a poor manager. We also know that this new manager is struggling with the new responsibilities that having a team brings; they're worried about losing friends and/or people thinking they're that idiot manager that no one likes. However, there are things this person can do to ameliorate these problems, one of which is to talk (and listen) to their team members, another of which is to have an outside, independent person to talk to (you!).

Mumpreneur – your recap might be; mums in business have possibly the best reason of all to build a business, however, what we know is that 80% of small businesses fail in the first 18 months. The main reason that businesses fail is that they don't sell enough of their product or service to survive, and the reason they don't can often be negative feelings around actually finding customers and selling to them. Selling isn't the grubby experience that many fear; in fact, done properly, selling is simply an extension of excellent customer service. This ICA can define her own ICA, someone who can and will pay for her product/service and who is going to love it. This process is always easier with an independent person to bounce ideas off (a coach!).

Retiree – your recap might be; retirement is a massive pivot point in most people's lives, and like any major life change, it can bring a significant amount of stress with it. The number of people who talk positively about retirement, whilst secretly dreading it is much higher than you might think. Retirement doesn't have to be when you reach your sell-by date, it can, if approached in the right way, be a massively liberating experience. This ICA may be able to turn their feelings around by talking to their partner about how they feel and together they can create a plan for a new routine and way of life. This can be made significantly easier if they know what they want out of retirement, and that clarity is easier to find if there's an independent person to talk to (a coach!).

My content aimed at Stella says this: That we've established that the vast majority of coaches fail to create financially sustainable coaching businesses. We've also seen that the reason for this is that the business development ideas shared by the majority of coach training establishments is nowhere near detailed enough. We've understood that business development skills are a full 50% of the skills required to build a coaching business and we've also understood that most coaches don't have those skills. In addition, we've looked at the fastest route to having a successful coaching business, and that is to have a well-defined ICA, and I've talked about why that's the case. I've also offered help and support via our online community, Coaching Republic.

This is not a place to start waxing lyrical about how fabulous coaching is. In fact, the whole marketing message avoids talking about coaching, because coaching is the process, and people don't buy processes, as previously discussed. This recap is simply to remind your audience what you have said.

10 – Call To Action

Again (and I know I'm going on about this) you are not going to sell coaching. Please, if it's one of the only things you remember from this whole book, remember this; trying to sell coaching *by describing the process of coaching,* is the fastest way to become one of the 82% who fail.

The call to action section of the marketing message is very simply the place where you tell your audience what to do next. You tell them how to connect with you, in order for them to be able to take the ideas you've discussed/written about further.

Give your audience (whether in a spoken presentation, or on social media) a single instruction for your call to action. Too often, I see coaches saying *you can contact me on 07123 456789, or by email at coach@email.com, or find me on LinkedIn, and my website is fabulouscoach.com* and what I know to be true is that if you give people too many options, they do what all slightly confused people do; nothing.

Give potential clients a single way to contact you.

For example, I am fairly prolific on LinkedIn. I post multiple times a day and I give a single call to action. I say *'here's a link to my online scheduler, why don't we have a chat?'.* If I'm delivering a talk, I suggest that people come and book a coffee with me so we can have a chat about their coaching business.

Your Toolkit

When you've finished all the work that's described in this chapter, you have everything you need to use as a toolkit for every bit of marketing you do. From writing social media posts, to articles and blog posts; from podcasts to videos. Everything your client needs to hear has been defined in this chapter.

That's a relief, right?

Liz O'Neill – Case Study

Liz O'Neill is a technology leader within the charities sector. She's had a 20+ year career in technology leadership. Liz wanted to add coaching to her repertoire of skills, so that she could develop her teams and so she took a coaching qualification. Liz discovered that she loves coaching so much, she wondered about the feasibility of having a coaching business.

What follows is Liz in her own words, from an interview we had together.

Tell Me About Liz

Liz said:

I've worked in technology for nearly 20 years. It sounds incredible to say 20 years, to be honest. I took a computer science degree and then started work as a developer. I moved very quickly into project management and then into people management.

Fast forward about 18 years or so, I've had loads and loads of experience with managing really big technical teams; software developers and list testers, that kind of thing. As I managed quite big teams and some quite quirky personalities, I was looking to up my skills as a technical leader I wanted to be able to support my team a bit more. That's where the coaching came in for me. I wanted to be able to help my team, to coach and develop them. What I really wanted to do was to help them achieve their career goals. So I took a coaching qualification.

How Liz Found The Coaching Revolution

When I first started my coaching qualification, it wasn't really with the intention of being a full-time coach. It was simply to help me in the technical leadership role that I currently do. And then I had a bit of an epiphany. I was coming to the end of the course and I was sitting there, and I realised that coaching is the best part of my job. It's the bit I love. It's the bit that drives my purpose and my passion.

I had this wonderful moment where it occurred to me that I could actually do the bit of my job that I love the best as a full-time thing! I realise that this might sound really silly, but it simply hadn't occurred to me before and it was a light bulb moment.

My very next thought was that I know nothing about sales! I know nothing about running a business either. I know nothing about how to market, or how to sell myself as a coach. In short, I'm utterly clueless about anything about business!

I did quite a lot of research online and looking at various options and chance (fate?) led me to your website.

What Did You Want From The Coaching Revolution?

I wanted to make a go of my coaching business. I wanted to see if it is actually possible to create a coaching business. I'm a great believer in making sure that you have the help and support you need to do whatever it is you want to do, whether it's building your own business or learning a skill, or whatever it is. I wanted to make sure I gave myself the best chance of success.

I truly believe that the only way to succeed is with the right people around you. I suppose that's what I wanted really, I wanted to give myself the best opportunity I possibly could to make a go of building a coaching business. I've never done it and I didn't really know how to do it. I needed to engage with people that did know how to do it. That's exactly it; find somebody that's done it and get some help. So I found you.

What Did You Get From The Coaching Revolution?

I got so much more than I expected. When I first joined I thought I was going to get some coaching, some mentoring, some steps to take and a framework to hang it all one.

What I actually got was a team, I got support, I got an entire community of people who believe in me. I got the most amazing mentor and coach, not just in my own personal mentor, but the whole group of coaches. I got people that helped me achieve something that, in my heart-of-hearts, I didn't really think was possible.

I also got something that I'm really passionate about. I got to share some of the things that I know quite a bit about. I got to share my knowledge with other people. One of the most profound moments for me was our first face-to-face event in Birmingham. Paul (Snell) did a presentation and workshop about discovering your superpower. After some work, I realise that mine is sharing knowledge with intent. That's what I've been able to do as part of this most amazing group as well, is being able to share some of my knowledge with intent, which is really important to me.

The community that The Coaching Revolution has created is wonderful. It's a sharing culture. One of the things I was very nervous about is that I'm a real people person. I like having people around me. I like talking to people. I was worried that when you work for yourself, it can be really lonely. However, I'm not lonely – I have a whole community who have my back.

What Was Unexpected About Working With Us?

My ideal client is a technical leader, and because of that, they're embedded within a corporation. What that means is that they are quite difficult to reach, and even more difficult to actually engage as a corporate coaching client.

The lead time between the first engagement and actually signing up a client can be anywhere between about three and six months. So that was a real surprise to me. I think I was a bit naïve, I thought I'd have a conversation, they'd sign me up to coach their teams and that would be that. I had completely overlooked the procurement process that I'd have to go through, which is odd, because I work with it every day in my day job.

I also discovered that there's a level of tenacity involved with staying consistent with your message and your marketing efforts, even when it feels like nothing is working.

What Was The Best Thing About Working With Us?

There were I think there were a couple of little milestones that happened that made me realise that this was working. The first one was when people were reacting to me and sending me messages about something I'd post on LinkedIn or a talk that I'd delivered. That was the first sign that all my effort wasn't for nothing, there are conversations coming from this effort. Obviously the biggest 'wow' for me was signing my first coaching client.

Another point worth mentioning is that I had designed and published a website – I'm a techy, I find that sort of thing easy – but I realised very quickly from the initial work I did with my mentor, that this isn't the way that my client will connect with me, and so I stopped spending time on it. I've not even looked at it in ages. Without The Coaching Revolution, I could have spent literally hundreds of hours on it and they would have been wasted.

I think that's the best thing about The Coaching Revolution. It teaches you how to get clients, not how to do a whole load of other stuff that is not going to add any value and is not going to get you to where you want. All that other stuff can come later. It doesn't need to happen yet because you just don't need it now.

What Was The Most Challenging Thing About Working With Us?

Without doubt, it was about selling. Right before my first client signed their contract you and I had a conversation Sarah. We spoke on the phone about how to talk to this potential client becoming an actual client. I had a good idea of what I was going to say, but you suggested some alternative things I might want to consider, so I used them instead when the client and I spoke.

I know that simply by changing the words in the conversation I had with them, from what I was going to say, to what you suggested I say, was what got them over the line. Best of all, they didn't sign for one session, they signed for eight sessions. I'm talking about a corporate client paying for all eight sessions up front. Done, dusted. I was delighted!

I think the other one that sticks out for me is to do with my confidence. I'm used to doing presentations. I'm used to standing up in front of people. I'm used to managing big teams, but that has always been on technical subjects. The idea of standing up and selling me as a person was quite scary really. With my coaching business, I couldn't hide behind an organisation or a job title. That I actually have the confidence to stand up and deliver my marketing message as a presentation, to people who fit my ideal client profile *and have them become my clients on the back of it* has been amazing.

How Do You Feel About The Future?

The future is rosy.

The future's really exciting. It's still a little bit scary. At some point I know I'm going to have to jump from my full-time job, because I'm just getting so busy now that it's becoming a struggle, to balance my job and my business, even though I love them both. I think that's the next step for me. The fact I've reached this point in under a year is astonishing. I have to pinch myself and say 'hey, this is actually happening!'

What Would You Say To Those Who Are Thinking About Working With Us?

One of the reasons why I agreed to do this interview is because I wanted to be able to say to anybody who is reading this book; this works. This really, really works. You can honestly build a coaching business using what The Coaching Revolution teaches.

Your challenge is going to be consistency. Your challenge is going to be actually doing the work. If you do the work, it works. and it won't work unless you do the work.

Our community will support you when you're having a bad day, and you don't think that all your efforts are working, and you're trying your hardest and it's just not happening. Being able to talk to somebody and say *I need some help. This is not working. Can you look at this and tell me what I'm doing wrong?*

You can't do that on your own. You just can't. But you can do it with The Coaching Revolution. And you'll love it. We all do.

Be Where Your Client Is

Now that you know who you want to coach and you know what they need to hear in order to be able to understand the benefit of working with you, you need to figure out where they are, both online and offline.

What you need to realise here is that you can have the most perfectly crafted ICA and KNP and if you then send your message into the world in places where your ICA can't hear you, you've wasted all that time and effort. For this process to work, you simply **have** to figure out where your ICA hangs out.

This is the chapter in which I'm going to talk about social media, networking, and public speaking. Each of these has its place, but if the idea of public speaking makes you weak at the knees, you don't have to do it. However, I have to say that finding opportunities to speak, and then actually speaking there, is a quick way to gain credibility.

Finding where your ideal client is, is about understanding them so well that you know where they are on and offline. This is why you did all the work in the chapter on ideal clients and I (still) appreciate that you may have been quite resistance to doing that work. There is always resistance from coaches, so be reassured that you're not alone if I'm talking about you.

If you found yourself rolling your eyes and thinking *for crying out loud, this isn't necessary!* when you read the ICA chapter, I'm hoping that you've started to see just how necessary that work is.

Just a quick note here; if you haven't done that ICA work, go back and do it now, because understanding where your client is, depends entirely on this work.

Finding That ICA

Let me give you some examples of what I'm talking about:

New manager – this ICA could be on LinkedIn, as part of their professional life (depending upon the industry and sector they work in).

If you know which industry they work in (ICA work again) then you'll understand if this is where they're likely to be. If they are on LinkedIn, then this is a good place for you to be as well. They might also be on Instagram and so you may need to be on Instagram too. What you need to remember about Instagram (or Snapchat, or any of the other places where young, new managers might be) is that both Instagram and Snapchat are much more informal. People hanging out there tend not to be there with their 'work head' on. On LinkedIn, for example, you can talk about this ICA's world of work and the issues that they face using content from your KNP work. You can also talk about the outcomes that they can expect from working with you. Remember, you need to touch their emotions in your writing, and you need to clearly demonstrate that a) they're not alone, b) you understand completely and

c) help is available to them. On Instagram, you would talk more about their lifestyle, the outcomes that they can expect when working with you and of course you have to remember to choose your images wisely to reflect this.

Offline, this person may be at networking events. They probably won't be at a local small business networking event, they're far more likely to be at professional networking event and the ones that they'll be at depends entirely on what industry they work in.

You also need to consider what conferences that new managers in this industry attend, then you need to be there too. You don't necessarily want to exhibit (that can cost a fortune), but attending, with an open mind and a pocket full of business cards could be a really good use of your time.

One of our clients had recognised that his ICA would be exhibiting (in great numbers) at a particular event, so he bought a ticket to that event for the princely sum of £15 and spent his whole day chatting to the exhibitors in their quiet times. He wasn't trying to get sales from these conversations, those exhibiting were not in the market to be customers that day. However, he left the event with a diary full of 1:1 conversations booked to take place over the following weeks.

Mumpreneur – figuring out where this ICA hangs out may actually depend on the age of her children (which you have, of course, defined in your work on this ICA). For example, many primary school aged children in the UK get a copy of *Primary Times* at the end of each half term and so that may be a place you want to get an article, an advertisement or some editorial. If those children are secondary school age or older, then having a presence in the Primary Times is a waste of your time, effort and money.

Interestingly, this ICA is reasonably easy to find offline, because there are many networking events that either take place during the school day or take place with pre-school children attending too. Lining up speaking opportunities can be easily achieved as most networking events look for speakers, although be aware that you may be required to become a member in order to get the opportunity to speak. Also be aware that lots of networking events for mum business owners take place at venues that allow small children to attend – think soft-play places. What that means to you is that if you're speaking there, take your ***big*** voice with you!

Online, this ICA will almost certainly be on Facebook, because there are many, many Facebook groups set up for this ICA specifically. The UK-based ones that spring to mind include the Mums In Business Association (MIBA), which exists on and offline and BizMums – a UK organisation – which also exists on and offline. If you're not UK-based, you need to do some research.

Retiree – This ICA can be slightly more difficult to find, because the work 'retiree' covers a massive demographic. Depending upon the industry in which the retiree worked (or is still working) then they may well be on LinkedIn. They are possibly also on Instagram and Facebook. I say possibly on Instagram, because although Instagram has a user-base that is predominantly under 30, around 10% of all Instagram users are aged over 55 and that's millions of people!

Finding this ICA in the real world also depends entirely upon the ICA work you've done. You might need to think about what hobbies they have, or what hobbies they may have promised themselves they're going to take up and therefore, where might they be meeting people with similar interests. For example, if you're in Britain and your retiree ICA is a woman, perhaps she might be at the Women's Institute? (Please note, I'm aware that the WI has members who are not retirees!) The WI welcomes speakers. If you're not in the UK, I'm sure there are similar organisations in other countries, you need to do your research in the country where you're based.

Once you are where your ICA is, you need to talk to them in a way that's going to make them think *s/he's talking about me!* I know I keep saying this, but to reiterate, this is how you generate that holy grail of inbound inquiries. These inbound inquiries come from clever use of the content of your KNP.

For example, you could share a meme (with a meaningful quote) on Instagram, or Facebook, or LinkedIn or any social media platform. Remember; using meaningful quotes has to be approached carefully. Any quote you use needs to be very carefully targeted at your ICA and not that 'hopeful marketing' that I mentioned earlier, where coaches post 'coach' things like 'dream big and you will achieve' etc.

If you're scratching your head and thinking I have absolutely no idea where my ICA is, then you need to do one of two things (or both of them!).

1. Go back to the chapter on creating an ideal client and do the work. Stop getting hung up on the fact that the ICA isn't a real person and *make* them real. You should, by

now, have understood why it's so important that they are real people, with real problems and real feelings. Those are things you will use to hone your marketing message and deliver it in the right place.

2. Put some research in and find the demographics of various social media platforms as well as where your ICA is offline. You need to get this right and to get it right requires work. You know your ICA far better than anyone else, in fact, you should know and understand them as well as you understand your best friend. Once you have this relationship with them, working out where they are on and offline becomes a matter of actual research, rather than guess work.

Can I remind you that I never promised this work would be easy, I said it would be simple, and it is simple. It is also however, a significant piece of work.

In order to discover which social media platform your ICA is on will involve some sleuthing. Your job as the marketing department of your coaching business is to find out where your ICA is, if you don't already know.

Social Media

Different social media platforms have different audiences and you need to choose the social media platform where your ICA is most likely to be. I've spoken to countless coaches who have said things like *'oh, I don't use social media'* or *'I hate LinkedIn'* or *'I've never used Instagram, I'm just not interested'.*

The bottom line is this; once again it's not about you. It is, like absolutely everything else, about where your ICA is. If they're on LinkedIn, then you too must be on LinkedIn. If they're on Instagram then you may have some learning to do. It is vital that you do this, because otherwise you're *wasting your time*.

Let me explain what I mean; if you are a coach who wants to work within the corporate world, your ICA will be embedded within that corporate structure. Chances are, that ICA won't be using Facebook with their 'corporate' head on. They'll be in 'out of office' mode when they're browsing Facebook. It's far more likely that your ICA is going to be on LinkedIn when they have their corporate – and therefore 'work' – head on, because LinkedIn is a virtual professional network. Your ICA will be more receptive to your message (which you will have pulled from your marketing toolkit – the thing you have created in previous chapters) if they read it in 'work mode'.

I would like to take a moment to emphasise what I just said. This exercise isn't to find out which social media platforms your ICA is on. It is specifically to deduce which social media your ICA is on *and in the right mindset to receive your message*. The frame of mind that they're in when on any given platform will help inform you of where you need to be. In short, you need your ICA to be in the frame of mind that suits the kind of coaching you offer.

Frame Of Mind

Let me expand, briefly, on what I mean by your ICA being in the right frame of mind to hear your message.

Let me give you an example or two:

If you're a life coach, who works with adventurers, to help them plan and achieve their next big adventure, then you need to be wherever they are, when they're in their excited, adventurous state of mind. Perhaps that's Instagram, because there are millions of fabulous images of the world to whet their appetite on Instagram.

If you're a life coach who works with young women to help them get past an 'is this it?' moment in their lives. You need to figure out where they are, when they're feeling this the most. Is it LinkedIn, Instagram, or perhaps it's SnapChat?

Social Media Demographics

I know this is a bit of a minefield and so I've provided the next chapter, which is full of statistics to give you some insight into social media facts and figures. You can use these statistics to help you decide where your ICA is.

Once You've Found Your Client

Once you know which social media platform(s) your client is on, your job is to connect with as many people who look like your ideal client as possible. My ideal client is a qualified coach and they're on LinkedIn, so I search for various coaching qualifications, and send connection requests to people who have them on their profiles. I also search for the word coach, and then eliminate sports coaches.

You need to figure out what your ICA's job title is, or how they describe themselves. Again, it's not about you and what you think they should be called, or should call themselves, it's about how *they* describe themselves.

On Facebook, it may be that you need to join groups in which your ICA hangs out. Add value to the group, and your ICA will start to notice you; you'll become visible to them. Do not hop into a Facebook group and spam the life out of it with a 'buy my coaching' message, over and over again, share your wisdom and knowledge and they will notice. Remember, your wisdom and knowledge come from your marketing toolkit!

Social Media Statistics

I've put this chapter here to keep the facts and figures stuff together and away from the rest of my book. I've done this for two reasons.

Firstly, not everyone is interested in facts and figures and if you fit that category, come back and dip into this chapter to find the statistics on the particular social media platform you're researching.

Secondly, this chapter interferes with the 'flow' of the book and so I wanted to make it into a discreet chapter. It's not me talking to you, it's a whole bunch of data. Admittedly, it's interesting data – or I think so anyway – but it is simply data.

The following data is gleaned from various places, but particularly from Omnicore's website (a USA-based, reputable digital marketing agency) and is correct at April 2019. For the record, the data is USA-centric, but extrapolates well.

Facebook

Founded by Mark Zuckerberg and his fellow Harvard students in 2004, Facebook was originally called TheFacebook and was created purely to allow Harvard students to network online.

It quickly expanded to include other colleges in the Boston area. Then, in September 2006 anyone over the age of 13 with a valid email address could create an account.

The Numbers

- Total Number of Monthly Active Users: 2.41 billion
- Total number of Mobile Daily Active Users: 1.59 billion
- Facebook Stories Daily Viewers: 500 million

Demographics and other user statistics

- Facebook users are **43% female and 57% male**
- *Of all the people on the internet,* **83% of Women & 75% of Men** use Facebook
- Average Facebook user has **155 'friends'**
- 62% of online Seniors **aged 65+** are on Facebook and 72% are between **age 50-64**
- 88% of online users of **age 18-29** are on Facebook, 84% of those **30-49**
- 82% of college graduates are on Facebook
- 72% of online users of **income more than $75K** are on Facebook
- **85% of Facebook's daily active users** come from outside the US/Canada
- The largest population on Facebook is from India with over **270 million users** followed by 190 million from the U.S.
- Brazil and Indonesia both have around **120 million users**
- Monthly Active Users from Asia are **1 billion**
- Europe has **385 million Facebook users**
- 96% of Facebook users **accessed via mobile devices**

Fun Facts

- Facebook accounts for over 42 percent of monthly social media visits
- **5 billion** comments are left on Facebook pages monthly
- 42% of customer service responses happen during the first 60 minutes
- The Facebook like button has been pressed **1.13 trillion times**
- As of January 2016, 100 million hours of video was watched on Facebook daily
- The average time spent on Facebook per visit is 35 minutes up from 20 minutes previously
- Every 60 seconds there are 317,000 status updates; 400 new users; 147,000 photos uploaded; and 54,000 shared links
- **More than 83% of daily active users are outside the US and Canada** the number has grown from 75% in the previous year which goes on to show the increased growth in the rest of the world
- Facebook Gets Over 8 Billion Average Daily Video Views.
- **85% of Facebook users watch videos with the sound off**
- Captioned video ads can increase video view time by an average of 12%
- 80% of users are annoyed when videos auto-play sound, and it gives them a negative impression of your brand
- 350 Million photos are uploaded every day, with 14.58 million photo uploads per hour, 243,000 photo uploads per minute, and 4,000 photo uploads per second
- 20% of videos are live broadcasts.
- Every 20 Minutes, 1 million links are shared, 20 million friend requests are sent, and 3 million messages are sent.
- 55 million status updates are made every day.

- Facebook is available in 101 languages with over 300,000 users helping in translation.
- Facebook app has been downloaded 107 million times via Google Play.
- 1 billion people use Facebook groups.
- 75 million Facebook users use Watch at least one minute per day.
- Most followed person on Facebook is Cristiano Ronaldo with 122 million subscribers.
- 36% of top stories on Facebook are related to politics.
- There are 120 million fake users on Facebook.
- On average, Americans spend 38 minutes per day on Facebook.
- 87% of co-workers connect using Facebook.
- 74% of Facebook users visit the site daily.

Instagram

Launched in 2010, Instagram exploded onto the social media scene. It grew to a million users in just two months. Facebook bought Instagram in 2012 for $1 billion.

The Numbers

- Total Number of Monthly Active Instagram Users: 1 billion +
- Total Number of Daily Active Instagram Users: 500 million +
- Instagram Stories Daily Active Users: 500 million +
- Number of Photos Shared to Date: 50 billion +
- Number of Businesses on Instagram: 25 million +
- Number of Instagram Likes per day: 4.2 billion
- Number of Photos & Videos uploaded per day: 100 million+

Demographics and other user statistics

- 52% of Instagram users are Females and 42% are male.
- 110 million Instagram users are from the US.
- Instagram is used by 43% of American women and 31% of men.
- 37% of US adults use Instagram and the United States has the biggest number of Instagram users.
- Six in ten online adults have Instagram accounts.
- 32% of all Internet users are on Instagram.
- 31% of internet users between the ages of 18 and 24 use Instagram and 32% of internet users between the ages of 25 and 34 use Instagram.
- 72% of teens use Instagram.
- 130 million Instagram accounts tap on a shopping post to learn more about products every month.
- 35% of US teenagers say Instagram is their **preferred social media platform.**
- 63% of Americans use Instagram daily.
- 200 million+ Instagrammers visit at least one business profile daily.
- There are 500,000 active influencers on Instagram.
- 69% of US marketers plan to spend most of their **influencer budget** on Instagram.
- **Instagram's revenue** is expected to reach $14 billion dollars.
- 1/3 of the most viewed stories are from businesses.
- 78% of influencers prefer Instagram for brand collaboration.
- User-Generated Content Has a **4.5% higher conversion rate.**
- 55.4% of Influencers use Instagram Stories for Sponsored campaigns.

- The potential reach of advertising on Instagram is 802 million.
- Instagram's projected revenue in 2019 is **$14 billion**

Fun Facts

- Instagram is 6th most popular social network worldwide.
- Most liked photo on Instagram is a photo of an egg with 53.6 million likes
- More than 50 billion photos have been uploaded to Instagram so far.
- 50% of Instagram users use explore page every month.
- Posts with a location get **79% more engagement**
- **7 out of 10 hashtags** on Instagram are branded.
- 60% of people say they discover new products on Instagram.
- 70%of shopping enthusiasts turn to Instagram for product discovery.
- **Photos with faces** get 38% more likes.
- Posts with at least one hashtag average **12.6% more engagement**
- Most-used giphy sticker in stories is *heart love sticker* by Arata.
- Most-used face filter in stories is *heart eyes*
- Brazil ranked second in female user share, the country is home to the largest total Instagram user base in Latin America and second worldwide.
- Instagram users **engage more on weekdays** with Tuesday and Thursday showing most engagement.
- **50% of Instagram** captions and comments contain emojis.
- Instagram videos get over twice the engagement than Instagram photos.
- The **most popular hashtags** on Instagram are #Love,

#Instagood, #Photooftheday, #Fashion, and #Beautiful

- Pizza is the most Instagrammed food globally, followed by Sushi
- Instagram influencers are charging up to $100,000 for a sponsored post
- 68% of people come to Instagram to **interact with creators**
- 50% of Sponsored feed posts last year **originated in the U.S.**
- **IGTV app** has 4.2 million installs worldwide

Instagram for Business

- An estimated **71% of US businesses** are on Instagram in 2018
- Instagram now has more than 2 million monthly advertisers and **25 million business**

LinkedIn

LinkedIn was an early entry to the social networking platforms, although to be fair it considers itself to be a professional networking platform. It was started in 2002 (and launched to the world in 2003) by venture capitalist Reid Hoffman, along with a cohort of marketers and techies. It became profitable in 2007, by which point it had 15 million users. By 2010, that number was 100 million. In 2016, it was bought by Microsoft.

The Numbers

- Total number of Linkedin users: 630 million
- Total number of monthly active Linkedin users: 303 million

- Percentage of Linkedin monthly active users: 48.1%
- Number of new Linkedin members **per second**: 2

Linkedin Demographics

- More than 70% of Linkedin users are from Outside the U.S.
- 90 million LinkedIn users are senior level influencers and 63 million are in decision-making positions
- 40 million students and recent college graduates on LinkedIn
- There are 57% of male users and 43% female users on LinkedIn
- After US, India, Brazil, Great Britain and Canada have the highest number of Linkedin users
- 25% of millennials (18-24 years old) use Linkedin
- There are **87 million millennials** on LinkedIn with 11 million in decision-making positions
- 28% of all male internet users use Linkedin, whereas 27% of all female internet users use Linkedin
- 49% of Linkedin users earn more than $75,000 in a year
- 51% of US college graduates use LinkedIn
- 190 million workers in the U.S. have Linkedin profiles
- 11% of adults aged 18+ can be reached with adverts on Linkedin

Linkedin Content Marketing

- LinkedIn is the #1 channel 94% of B2B marketers use to distribute content
- Of 500 million users, just 3 million users share content weekly
- LinkedIn makes up more than 50% of all social traffic to

B2B websites & blogs

- 91% of marketing executives list LinkedIn as the top place to find quality content
- 92% of B2B marketers include LinkedIn in their digital marketing mix
- Only **1 million users** have published an article on LinkedIn
- About 45% of LinkedIn article readers are in upper-level positions (managers, VPs, Directors, C-level)
- **How-to & list posts perform the best on LinkedIn**
- Posts split into **5, 7, or 9 headings** perform the best
- Articles with **titles between 40-49 characters** perform the best on LinkedIn
- **Articles without video perform better** than those with video
- **80% of B2B leads** come from LinkedIn vs. 13% on Twitter & 7% on Facebook

Fun Facts

- **41% of millionaires** use LinkedIn
- There are 50,000 skills listed on LinkedIn
- Top soft skill on LinkedIn is **creativity** and top hard skill on LinkedIn is **cloud computing**
- LinkedIn now has over **30 million companies** on LinkedIn with **20 million open job listings**
- There are 90,000 schools listed on Linkedin
- 27% of US Adults say they use LinkedIn
- There are **100 million job applications** on LinkedIn every month
- 1 million professionals have published a post on LinkedIn
- An average user spends 17 minutes monthly on Linkedin
- Motivated was the **most used word** on Linkedin in 2014
- LinkedIn **profiles with professional headshots** get **14**

times more profile views

- Statistical analysis and data mining are top skills on Linkedin
- **59% of Linkedin members** have never worked at a company with more than 200 employees
- There are 5.5 million accountants on LinkedIn
- There are 3 million MBA graduates on LinkedIn
- There are 6 million IT decision makers on LinkedIn
- **79% of B2B marketers** see LinkedIn as an effective source of lead generation
- **UK & India are the fastest growing markets** on LinkedIn messaging
- There have been 11 billion endorsements on LinkedIn
- The average CEO has **930 connections**
- The most overused profile word continues to be **Motivated** – which also topped 2014 and 2015
- More than **90% of recruiters** use LinkedIn regularly
- **LinkedIn SlideShare** now has **80 million monthly active users**
- There are 17 million opinion leaders on LinkedIn

Twitter

Founded in 2006, Twitter is a micro-blogging site. Originally, small messages 'Tweets' could be just 140 characters long. In 2017 that was increased to 240 characters for most languages.

The Numbers

- Total Number of Monthly Active Twitter Users: 330 million
- Total Number of Tweets sent per Day: 500 million

- Number of Twitter Daily Active Users: 139 million

Demographics and other user statistics

- 34% of Twitter users are females and 66% are males
- 22% of US adults use Twitter
- 24% of All male internet users use Twitter, whereas 21% of all female internet users use Twitter
- There are 262 million International Twitter users (users outside the US) which make up 79% of all Twitter accounts
- There are 68 million monthly active Twitter users in the US
- Roughly **42% of Twitter users** are on the platform daily
- The total number of Twitter users in the UK is **14.1 million**
- 37% of Twitter users are between the ages of 18 and 29, 25% of users are 30-49 years old
- 56% of Twitter users $50,000 and more in a year
- 80% of Twitter users are **affluent millennials**
- The top three countries by user count outside the U.S. are Japan (36.7 million users), Saudi Arabia (9.9 million), and Turkey (8.6 million)
- 38% of Americans aged 18 to 29 years old use Twitter
- 80% of Twitter users accessing the platform on a mobile device, and 93% of video views are on mobile

Fun Facts

- Twitter can handle 18 **quintillion** user accounts (I didn't even know that was a number!)
- 74% of Twitter users say they use the network to get their news
- 85% of small and medium business users use Twitter to provide customer service
- More than 100 million tweets contained GIFs in 2015

- Saudi Arabia has the highest percentage of internet users who are active on Twitter
- In Q3 2017, Twitter live-streamed more than **830 events**
- Twitter also live-streamed 96 million hours of live user-generated content in Q3 via Periscope
- Number of Twitter timeline views in 2014 is 200 billion
- 83% of 193 UN member countries have a Twitter presence
- Twitter's revenue per employee is $488,913
- Most followed person on Twitter is Katy Perry with 107.47 million followers
- 93% of Twitter's video views happen on a mobile device
- **Discover something new and interesting** is the **most cited reason** for visiting twitter
- Twitter app got 11.7 million downloads from the AppStore
- Most used emoji in tweets is "Face with Tears of Joy" (used more than two billion times)

Pinterest

Pinterest was founded in 2009 by Ben Silbermann and went live in 2010 as an invitation only, image-sharing site. It officially launched in 2011 and had 10,000 users within 9 months. At this time, it also introduced an iPhone app, (which was both exciting and fairly unusual at the time). Pinterest made it to the list of the "50 Best Websites" published by Time Magazine in August 2011.

The Numbers

- Total Number of Monthly Active Pinterest Users: 300 million+

- Number of Pinterest Users from the US: 85 million
- Number of Pinterest Users around the World: 50%+
- Total Number of Pinterest Pins: 200 billion
- Total Number of Pinterest Boards: 4 billion
- Total Number of Pinterest Users who save Shopping Pins on Boards Daily: 2 million

Demographics and other user statistics

- 70% of Pinterest users are females
- 40% of new signups are men; 60% are women
- Men account for only 7% of total pins on Pinterest
- 50%+ Pinners live outside the U.S.
- 34% of users aged 18-29 in the U.S. use Pinterest
- 42% of U.S. women adults use Pinterest
- 80% of U.S. mothers who use the internet use Pinterest
- Millennials use Pinterest as much as they use Instagram
- The median age of a Pinterest user is 40, however, the majority of active pinners are below 40
- Half of Pinterest users earn $50K or more per year, with 10 percent of 'Pinteresting' households making more than $125K
- 144.5 million – Number of people that Pinterest reports can be reached with adverts on Pinterest
- 28% of all U.S. social media users are Pinterest users.

Fun Facts

- There are over 75 billion ideas on Pinterest
- 40% of Pinners have a household income of $100k+
- 87% of Pinners have purchased a product because of Pinterest.
- 72% of Pinners use Pinterest to decide what to buy **offline**

- 1 in 2 Millennials Uses Pinterest Every Month
- Over 5% of all referral traffic to websites comes from Pinterest
- Pinterest says that **85% of its users access Pinterest through a mobile device**
- 93% of active pinners said they use Pinterest to plan for purchases and 87% said they've purchased something because of Pinterest
- **Two-thirds of pins** represent brands and products
- Food & Drink & Technology are the **most popular categories for men**
- An average Pins made by an active female user is 158
- The top category in the US is **Art, Art Supplies & Hobbies**
- Recipes: There are more than 1.7 billion recipe Pins
- Shopping: Every day nearly 2M people Pin product rich Pins
- 50% have made a purchase after seeing a promoted pin
- Promoted Pins are repinned an average of 11 times per advertisement
- Articles: More than 14 million articles are Pinned each day
- Average time spent on Pinterest per visit is 14.2 minutes
- 85% Pinterest users use the site when they want to start a new project
- 64% Pinterest users described the platform as a place to find ideas, products or services they can trust
- 47% Social media users saw Pinterest as the platform for discovering and shopping for products
- Average number of monthly searches on Pinterest is 2 billion
- 84% Pinners use Pinterest to decide what to buy
- 98% of people who use Pinterest have tried something new they found on Pinterest
- 77% of people who use Pinterest have found a new brand or product

Turn Conversations into Clients

As I've mentioned previously, our business development process generates inbound enquiries. That's the way marketers describe the process of your ICA thinking, *s/he's talking about me!* and then either sending you a message on social media or walking up to you after a live presentation and asking if they can have a chat with you. The enquiry is inbound in that it's literally (or virtually) walking up to you and asking to talk to you.

Inbound enquiries are the holy grail of any business. To have someone come to you and say *I've been listening to what you say and I think you can help me* is the ideal scenario for any coach. In fact, to go back to what I said in an earlier chapter of this book, it's actually what coaches believe is going to happen when they first qualify.

Turning those conversations into paying clients is a skill. It's one that coaches usually have in abundance. If I could have a penny for every coach who has said the following phrase to me I would have enough money to... well at least buy that decent coffee I mentioned earlier.

Once I'm talking to someone, I can show them the benefit of working with me. I just can't manage to create enough opportunities to do so coaches say. Taking that fabulous conversation and then actually asking for their money in order that you can coach them is a different matter.

Coaches can find that trying to craft a 'sales conversation' is something that they fret about. They worry that they'll seem pushy, they worry about rejection and (of course) they hate talking about money.

So let's break down this topic into its different mind monkeys and tackle them one at a time.

I Hate Selling

There is an odd view that persists to this day, that selling is somehow grubby. This view extends to marketing too and it seems to be validated by those who think it, around the idea that sales and marketing are somehow 'tricksy'.

The idea that salespeople, or marketing professionals are out to trick you into buying sub-standard rubbish, at a massively inflated price is a very old-fashioned view. In the 1980s and 90s, selling was given a bad name by people like time-share salespeople and those who sold second-hand cars etc. Those people did rip off unsuspecting customers. However, we're talking more than two decades ago!

In the intervening 20 years, that kind of sleazy sales patter has gone. Sales has moved – for the most part – into a respectable stage in the customer service journey.

What Is Selling?

Selling isn't the beginning of the customer service journey and it's not the end of it either. The actual sale comes somewhere around the middle of the journey.

The beginning of the journey starts with awareness that you even exist on the part of the potential client. Once they're aware you exist the next part of the journey is for them to become interested in what you do. Then, they desire to work with you and finally, they take action and buy your coaching. From that point forward, the journey is about your service delivery.

The end of the customer service journey is when your client successfully completes their coaching and they become raving fans.

To be clear, in our 21st century western society, nothing happens without a sale. Let me say that again (because this is important) *nothing happens without a sale*. There is precious little in this world that we don't pay for. I used to say that now we drink bottled water, only air is free. However, with the advent of air-conditioning it seems that in some locations, even air has a price.

Interestingly, we are never worried about sales or selling when we are on the other side of the equation. What I mean is that we are all perfectly comfortable buyers. We don't even think about it. We take part in monetary transactions constantly in our daily lives, from buying a pint of milk, to setting up a direct debit to pay for a utility, these are all financial transactions and ones with which we are very comfortable.

The discomfort comes when we're on the selling side and it's really odd. Think for one moment if those to whom we hand money over were squeamish about it. If the waiter in a restaurant didn't want to give you the bill, because he didn't like talking about money, or if the person on the supermarket checkout didn't want to give you the total price because they felt pushy. That would just be downright peculiar, right?

Money is simply a system of exchange, your knowledge and expertise in exchange for the client's money. As long as both of you feel that the amount of money being exchanged is fair, then no one will feel awkward. How much is fair? Fair is what your ICA thinks is fair. Fair is how much removing the problem that they have is worth to them.

Sales -v- Marketing

If you look at the description of the part of the customer service journey before the actual exchange of money, that part can be split into marketing and selling. Exactly where the line between the two comes is debatable and far greater minds than mine haven't really agreed where that line is. It doesn't actually matter though, because as people who own and operate our own businesses, we do all of it anyway, at least in the beginning.

What I've described above can be demonstrated by this acronym: AIDA

A = Awareness
I = Interest
D = Desire
A = Action

The action part is the sale. The D is the letter that causes arguments about whether it's sales or marketing. Honestly, who cares whether its sales or marketing? We will be doing all of it, so let's crack on. I go into much more detail about AIDA in the chapter called Rinse and Repeat, so I'll give you a brief explanation of the acronym and then move on from this topic.

Action

The action you want your ICA to take is to have a conversation with you. I do that by having an online scheduler and I share the link to this scheduler everywhere I show up. I am very specific about what I want my ICA to do, about the action that I want them to take. I say *this is a link to my diary, let's talk.* That's it. That's my call to action (CTA) and I use it at the end of almost every post and almost every article I write.

You need a specific, simple CTA because, believe it or not, people need to know what to do next and it's your job to tell them. If you want them on your email list, then the action you want them to take is to subscribe to your list, so ask them. I want to speak to people, so I share my diary link with an invitation to book an appointment at a time of their choosing.

If you don't use a CTA, you won't get people taking action. I know that seems absurd, but it's true. Equally, if you give people 4 or 5 different ways to contact you, they won't. Give people too many options and you confuse them. Confused people do nothing; in particular, they won't contact you. So whatever you do, don't say 'this is my phone number, my email address is this, you can send me a private message, my mobile number is 07123 456789, oh and I also respond to smoke signals and carrier pigeon' (!!)

Do say (for example)

- here's a link to my diary to book a convenient time to speak to me (I've covered tools in the chapter called Cool Tools)
- PM me to arrange a time to talk (PM = private message on LinkedIn or Facebook. It's DM – direct message – on Twitter)
- send me an email at my.email@address.com
- call me on 07123 456789

Recap

Let me just recap what's happened in your client journey. You've started to speak to your ICA online (and offline too possibly) and they have moved through the AIDA process.

Originally, your client had no idea that you existed. Then, they became aware of you in the periphery of their lives. You began to move from the periphery into their conscious mind as they became interested in what you do. Then, they started to become more interested in what you have to say. So interested in fact, that they found themselves wanting to understand more about you, and how you can help them. Finally, they took action and responded to your call to action.

Having That Conversation

I don't need to tell you how to conduct a coaching strategy session (I call this an initial coaching conversation by the way). You've got the delivery half of your business sorted after all, haven't you?

The way to segue from your initial coaching conversation, to a sales conversation that doesn't feel dreadful, is to take control of the end of the conversation. Let me explain.

What Does This Person Want?

As with all initial coaching conversations, you're going to focus on the client, and on what they want. Remember, that at this point, they've come to you because what you said about the specific problem they have, has resonated with them, so stick to that topic for now. In the future, when they're paying you to coach them, you can move onto all the whole spectrum of their lives, but for now, you have one single, very specific topic to unwrap.

Explore the topic with them. Work out where this problem they have manifests itself in their lives and what impact it is having in this particular individual. They may have lots in common with your ICA, but they are unique of course, so explore.

Find out how their lives would be without the problem they have. Discover exactly how much they want this new life, without the problem. Dig deep, find out everything.

Do not try to 'add value' by solving the problem that they have, *even if you can see where you think it could be solved.* That's not your role as either a coach, or in this case, the business development manager for your coaching business. If you offer a solution to the problem in the initial coaching conversation, then why would they need to work with you? They can simply go away and implement your ideas and/or suggestions.

When you reach the natural conclusion of the digging, and just as you will have done with other 'strategy' calls, you're going to talk about how working together might look.

Remembering that crazy waiter and supermarket check-out operator, you are simply going to state the price. You're not going to state the price and then immediately discount it. You're not going to apologise for it, you're simply going to tell them what the price is. Here are a few examples of what you might say:

- *Working with me costs £$XXX for XX sessions*
- *The fee for my programme is £$XXX*
- *The price for resolving this problem is £$XXX*
- *My X week programme costs £$XXX*

You are then going to ask them if they have any questions about the idea of working together. This is important. You'll often hear sales trainers talk about handling objections. If you do this my way, you'll rarely get any.

The reason you're asking them if they have any questions is because an 'objection' in a buying conversation is almost always there because the person who is interested in buying doesn't have enough information to make an informed decision. Asking them if they have questions allows them to find out the information that is missing from their understanding thus far.

The Secret Sauce

Once you've described what working together will look like, said the price, and answered all their questions, your next question to your potential client is this: *What would you like to happen next?*

Then **shut up.** Do. Not. Speak.
Wait.
Wait for them to speak. It's their turn to speak next.

The reason you're waiting is to give this person the space to process their thoughts. It's polite to do so. They need the bandwidth to consider everything you've talked about for the last hour, to contemplate their new lives, free of this problem, and to figure out how you fit into their world to make this happen.

They will either say yes they do want to work with you, or no they don't (yet!).

If they say yes, then they have done themselves a huge favour and will start to move towards a better life (we all know that's where coaching takes people).

If they say no, they are not rejecting you, they are simply choosing that this isn't the time for them to move towards a

better life, and that's their decision to make.
Neither a yes, nor a no is a reflection on you. As with all marketing, this simply isn't about you at all.

Make sure that by the time the initial coaching conversation has ended, you have given them the most wonderful experience of you and your coaching. Whatever their decision, you want to leave them feeling uplifted and optimistic.

Conversion Rates

The number of initial coaching conversations you have, divided by the number of yeses you get (to becoming your client), is your conversion rate.

I've been in sales for years and I've been doing the business development for The Coaching Revolution since we started and so I know for every two people I speak to I'll enrol one new mentee with The Coaching Revolution.

My conversion rate is 50%.

It wasn't always 50%. however, over time, and with experience, I now understand my ICA so well, that I know pretty much what they're going to say and how the problem that they have – no paying clients – is impacting them. With practice, my conversion rate has improved and yours will too.

What having a conversion rate means, is that I'm not panicking if someone says no. I know, with utter certainty, that over several conversations, that 50% of the people I'm talking to will want to become our client. It doesn't work in an alternate pattern of 'yes, no, yes, no', but the numbers don't lie. For every 20 conversations I have, 10 people will join us. It's just fact.

Your conversion rate will grow with practice. It will grow as you polish your marketing toolkit. Remember this, every initial coaching conversation you have with someone who fits your ICA profile will give you more ideas of what to say to your ICA in your marketing. Your understanding of your ICA, their problem and its various manifestations will grow and grow as you talk to more and more people who fit that profile.

Treat every conversation you have as not only an initial coaching conversation, but also a learning experience. You will learn so much about your ICA and the problems that they have from talking to them. Initial coaching conversations (aka buying conversations) are a goldmine for developing your understanding of your ICA.

Inserting Yourself Into The Process

Do not insert yourself into the process I have described above. What I mean by that is do not, under any circumstances make decisions on behalf of your potential client.

It is not your place to decide that a particular person can't afford coaching, for example. Coaches do this *all the time.* They say things like *I didn't want to be pushy* or *they couldn't afford coaching*, or *they had other, more pressing needs that they told me about.*

Those are simply not decisions for you to make. They are presumptions and, if this was happening the other way round you would be horrified.

Do Not Presume

Let me tell you a story.

When I was married and my children were small, my husband and I wanted to move from one area of Cumbria to another. We didn't really know the new area very well and so we decided that we'd rent in the new area for 6 months to give us an opportunity to get to know the area and find the perfect house to buy.

This was in the early 2000s and the internet was in its infancy. Certainly, estate agents didn't have websites at that point. The way houses to rent were advertised was in the local newspaper. I found an interesting looking barn conversion to rent. It was interesting, because although it was quite small, it had a cavernous, water-proof outbuilding which meant that we could store furniture there, rather than pay for storage. So, one wet and windy February afternoon, we took the dog for a long walk and ended up at the estate agent that was advertising this barn.

I was wearing my wax jacket and wellies. It was pouring down and my husband and I were drenched, but as this was our last port of call and we were off home for hot showers next, we weren't overly concerned.

To this day I'm not sure why I didn't just ask for details of the barn conversion to rent. Maybe I thought that there might be something else of interest, I'm not sure. However, what I asked the woman in the estate agents for, was details of 3-bed houses to rent please.

She looked me up and down and took from her filing cabinet details of a tiny terraced house in a poor part of town. The rent was about a third of our budget. I enquired about other properties to rent, and she told me that this was everything she had.

Confused, I asked her specifically about the barn-conversion I'd seen advertised in the local newspaper and asked for confirmation that it was no longer available. She looked flustered and started stammering.

The barn conversion was still available of course. The reason that the woman hadn't told me about any property other than the cheapest one that was available, was because she had taken one look at our bedraggled state and made a judgement call. She had decided what our budget was, and provided us with information that fitted her perception of us. I don't quite remember what I said to her, but I do remember the look of horror that crossed her face when she realised that not only had she made the wrong judgement, but she had also been caught out doing it. Needless to say, I have never, ever used that estate agent for anything since.

Do not presume to know your potential client's situation, financial or otherwise. Doing so is inserting yourself into the process. Specifically, it's inserting your mind monkeys into the process and doing this will prevent you from thriving.

Learning To Sell Is Like Learning To Drive

Do you remember when you learned to drive? I do. I remember particularly turning into a street that was about 500m in length and thinking *oh no! I have to get all the way up the gears,* ***and back down them*** *before I get to the end of this street!* I also remember bursting into tears at the top of Windermere village (in the English Lake District), when I had to do a hill start, and a right turn in a single manoeuvre.

I've driven hundreds of thousands of miles since then. I don't even think about gears, or street length, or hill starts, or anything other than road safety to be honest.

So it is with turning conversations into paying clients. Currently, this skill is outside your comfort zone and so every little aspect of it is magnified in terms of discomfort. You will agonise over every little thing and you'll overthink it. Take action anyway.

In taking action, you create data to work with. Data is knowledge and facts, and knowledge and facts are power. You also take the fear out of the process, one conversation at a time.

Keeping Hold Of The Ball

In the relationship you have with your potential client, the onus is upon you to keep hold of the conversational ball at all times.

The ball is a metaphor for control. You are the service provider; they are the potential customer. What that means is that it isn't their job to chase you, at all, for anything. It's *your* job to stay in control.

If you want to buy a new car, you will visit a dealer and ask all the questions you want to. The salesperson will take your details and it is their job to follow up with you. Can you imagine how frustrated (not to mention irritated!) you'd be if they left it to you to keep having to chase them?

Within an initial coaching conversation setting, if there is an action that your potential client needs to take, it's your job to put a framework around that. Let me give you an example of my own.

Our process for gaining mentees goes as follows:

- someone books an appointment to speak to me
- an email goes out automatically to confirm the time and date
- 24 hours before that appointment, another email goes out
- Jess (my coach coordinator) will send a text reminder the night before the appointment
- the potential mentee and I have a conversation
- at the beginning of the conversation, I give a framework for the conversation in that I say that if by the time we finish talking, we're in agreement that we're a good fit for one another, then I'll send them additional information
- at the end of that conversation, if we do feel like we're a good fit, I will send them an email with the additional information for them to digest

- I know that there will always be a question that I haven't answered in our additional information, so I always make an appointment for another conversation *before we get off the phone*
- we have a second conversation in which I answer all the questions the potential mentee has
- I'll then ask them *what would you like to happen next?* and shut up

Can you see how I keep hold of the ball all the way through this process? The biggest ball-holding part is that we don't get off the phone until I have a second conversation appointment in the diary. That's important. It isn't the responsibility of the potential mentee to find the answers to their questions, it's my responsibility to answer them.

It isn't the responsibility of your potential client to get back to you, it's your responsibility to get back to them. It's not pushy, it's good customer service.

Statistics Around Follow Up

The National Sales Executives Association (US-based) has a really interesting set of statistics. When you read this, substitute the word salespeople with coach, and the word prospect with potential coaching client.

> 48% of sales people never follow up with a prospect
> 25% of sales people make a second contact and stop
> 12 % of sales people make only three contacts and then stop
> Only 10% of sales people make more than three contacts

But:

2% of sales are made on the first contact
3% of sales are made on the second contact
5% of sales are made on the third contact
10% of sales are made on the fourth contact
80% of sales are made on the fifth to twelfth contact

Remember that your initial coaching conversation is not the first contact that your potential client has had with you. They will have seen and/or heard your marketing message a number of times before they contacted you.

What those statistics clearly demonstrate is that ‘pushy’ is nothing more than a mind monkey.

Jeff Matthews – Case Study

Jeff has a 30+ year career in banking, and 10+ years in property development and management. By the time Jeff joined us, he knew that he wanted a consulting and coaching business but wasn't sure how the marketing would work. He'd tried a few marketing activities and had no success and wanted to work with people who, as Jeff put it, know what they're doing.

What follows is Jeff in his own words, from an interview we had together.

Tell Me About Jeff

Jeff said:

I'm 58 years old, and I've been working since I was 16. I worked in banking for 31 years and while I was in this industry, I had a Eureka moment. Two things happened in the 90s which inspired me.

One of those things was that for a while, my job in the bank was in learning and development (L&D). During the time I worked in L&D, I found I loved delivering training. One time, the training course I was delivering had a strong coaching element in it, and I remember being enthralled and inspired by how powerful coaching can be.

Around about the same time there was a BBC television series called *Troubleshooter*. It was a series in which renowned British businessman Sir John Harvey Jones spent time with lots of different small companies, helping them to grow and solve problems, and I loved it! I really loved it.

My background in banking obviously means that I was used to working within a compliant, regulatory framework. I think I was already the entrepreneur trying to break out and push against the walls though. I thought I'd left it too long to breakout, but then, in 2008 I actually did start my own property investment company. I sold that in December last year and I'm now running my new consulting business with some property development in the background too.

Actual coaching is new to me, although I've wanted to learn more about it for some time now. What I really enjoy doing now is helping others and my new business means that I can do this.

How Jeff Found Us

I was scratching around really doing internet searches. I looked at several coaching franchises, but they weren't for me. They all had certain pitfalls, not least of which was the eye watering prices! More than that though, it just didn't feel right. Business development wise I was thinking, can I do this on my own or do I need help? I stumbled across one of your videos actually, doing a TEDx Talk and I was quite inspired by it. I was inspired to the point that I remember making an enquiry to The Coaching Revolution and thinking, 'This is interesting. Can we have a chat?'

We had an initial chat, and you sent me some more information. By the time we spoke for the second time, I wanted in. I think I realised that you can't just walk into being a coach. I know it's an unregulated industry, but I didn't want to be one of those people who call themselves a coach, but are making it up. I wanted to really develop good skills. What I now use is the ICF coaching framework all the time and both my clients and I love it.

What Did You Want From The Coaching Revolution?

I was hoping to strip things back to basics. I think I used the phrase 'debunk and reset' at the time. I also wanted to talk to somebody who had been in business for 40 years. I know I had that with Robert, my mentor. Effectively I wanted to talk to somebody who had been there, got the T-shirt, and effectively they were living what they were teaching, and living what they've done. That was really important to me because there's a lot of people out there at the moment who are peddling their wares for coaches or aspiring coaches who are not genuine.

I think the global statistic is that 18% succeed and not 82% will fail. I didn't want to be one of that 82%. I really wanted to speak to real honest, transparent people that knew what they were doing. I felt that straight away by talking to you. I talked to Paul too and I talked to a couple of people you were already working with and it just felt instinctively right. I'm very much a 'heart' person when it comes to decisions. I'm very instinctive, and it felt right, and for that reason I made the decision to come across you guys and I've enjoyed every minute. Absolutely loved it.

How Did You Find The ICF Credential Course?

I have to be honest and say that I was really worried about taking the ICF credential, as I haven't been in a classroom, virtual or otherwise, for over 20 years.

However, I absolutely loved it. Rachel, the course tutor is outstandingly good and I have loved every single minute.

What Did You Get From The Coaching Revolution?

I've had exactly what I hoped for and probably a bit more. I think one thing that struck me is, first of all, I must say that the right match with your mentor is important and you're so good at that matching. It was so important for me that I had a mentor that really understood the way I worked, and want to work, and I've absolutely had that.

Another thing I would say to answer your question fully, is that it's so easy just to sign up to a programme, take your 10 mentoring sessions, and think that's it. Most companies I looked at before I spoke to you did exactly that. However, life goes on. I love the fact that as Coaching Revolution client, I know for sure that in six months' time or 12 months' time,

I can actively participate with the community. I can still join the weekly online meet up, I can always attend the face-to-face events held during the year. I can also still pick up the phone to my mentor. He'll still be around, you're all still around. You're now my working colleagues and you're just there. That is very important to me.

The community goes beyond even that though. I think I've had conversations with probably half a dozen other coaches offline about either issues they have, or a question I may have for example. Best of all, that's happening outside the official process – it's an added bonus. I'm building my own personal support network of people who are doing what I do, in their own way and I am so grateful for that

What Was Unexpected About Working With Us?

I think the unexpected thing for me was that I didn't know as much as I thought I did!

Of course, we can all read books, and watch videos, but there's nothing like real-life support. As a secondary thing, I think it's important not to underestimate the importance of having an ideal client, and marketing message designed just for them. When I first heard of the concept, I was dubious, I'll admit.

However, I now know that having an ideal client, and the perfect marketing message for them is like having a secret map to success. It means you know exactly who you're looking for at things like networking meetings (I know my ideal client attends this kind of thing) and I don't have to feel like I need to persuade everyone I meet that I can help them.

A final unexpected thing I found is that historically, my sales experience has been very transactional and almost instant. The challenge I've got now is understanding that business generation can be a slow burn because you've got to build the trust. Somebody who's going to invest £$£$£ in me for 10 coaching sessions for example. That person isn't going to open up their soul to you during one 30-minute coffee meeting. As a coach, I've got to build that trust. I think what I'm saying is that the importance of being tenacious in your business development tactics can't be underestimated, but also being patient is equally important. I've had to readjust the way I approach business development, but guess what? It's working. I've got paying clients!

What Was The Best Thing About Working With Us?

Let me share a personal story with you. I hope that this will resonate with some of the people who are reading this. The best thing so far is doing this kind of work, and it's for a very personal reason.

Back in 2016, two things happened which really made me question what I wanted to do in my business life. One was my father became very ill, and he sadly passed away. The other one was the fact that in my property investment business I was very badly let down by a supplier. It really jolted me at the time when I was looking after my dad. To answer your question about what's the best thing that's happened; those two things really knocked me. I've found that the Coaching Revolution and the work I'm doing, has given me my mojo back. Before I found you, I'd spent 12 months thinking what am I going to do? What am I going to do for the next five, or ten years?

As I've already mentioned, I've wanted to do this kind of work since the 1990s. It was hidden deep within me. I'm so glad that I made the right decision about working with you, because it's given me the new lease of life I was looking for.

How Do You Feel About The Future?

I'm really optimistic. I'm optimistic because I'm always sandpapering away at my marketing techniques and message.

What I was doing before didn't work, and this just does. I'm gaining clients all the time; I've landed a prestigious contract with a large bank (not my old one) to mentor and coach their women in leadership and I'm excited about the way my business is going.

What Would You Say To Those Who Are Thinking About Working With Us?

I would definitely advocate that you go with a working partner like The Coaching Revolution. Don't go out and do it alone, because it's lonely, it takes longer to succeed and you're going to make mistakes that The Coaching Revolution can stop you making. Knowing what I now know, I don't believe that you can do this alone.

I checked out all those whom I believed were Coaching Revolution competitors, and I checked them out very carefully. I know that The Coaching Revolution is where my home is.

One other thing that I've already mentioned, but I'd like to reiterate; once you've had your mentoring sessions, it doesn't stop there. Some companies will take your money, they look after you for three, six months, whatever it is, and that's it. You're left to fly solo. No one in The Coaching Revolution is left to fly solo. Ever.

Rinse and Repeat

Consistency is vital in marketing, particularly in social media marketing.

What Does Consistency Look Like?

Consistency applies to two aspects of your marketing. Consistency in actually showing up, even when you don't want to (in fact especially when you don't want to) and consistency in your actual message.

Let's look at the latter first.

If you feel anxious about the ideal of offering one thing, to one kind of client, it's likely that your consistency in this area will be poor. We worked with a coach who wanted to offer coaching for women through the menopause, career coaching, coaching around burnout and coaching around retirement. She was unwilling to let go of any of these areas, even on a temporary basis, and so her results are not just mediocre, but actually pretty non-existent.

The problem with this coach's approach is that no one knows what she stands for. She's reasonably active on her social media platform of choice, but her message is not focused and so therefore is not clear. She is sharing four separate messages aimed at four separate kinds of potential client. The problem specifically is that people need to see you show up regularly, with the same message, before you actually become someone they want to engage with, let alone work with.

The coach in question doesn't want to let go of any of the areas of coaching about which she feels passionate, and I get that. She wants to help as many people as possible in areas that she knows that she can make a difference. The part that the coach is failing to realise is that by delivering an inconsistent message, she won't get clients, and this will mean she doesn't get to work with anyone at all, so can't make a difference anyway.

I know I've said this several times, and I'm saying it again: The important thing to remember is that you need to be known for **one** thing. You need to sell **one** thing, to **one** kind of client. Remember, this isn't forever, it's for *now*. You don't have to only ever market to one kind of person, but – and here's the thing – *you have to start somewhere*.

The whole point of this ideal client marketing concept is that you get a pipeline of inbound enquiries established and an income stream going. Once you have a solid income stream from one kind of client, that means you're well known for your one thing. At that point, you can tweak – but not before.

Do not be tempted to cast your net wide. I hope that the fact this chapter is towards the end of the book means that you already understand that, but just in case you don't, or you've somehow reverted to trying to market to 'anyone who...' let me give you a refresher.

Casting Your Net Wide

Every fibre in the beings of those who are not marketers shouts that casting your net wide so that you can work with anyone *has* to be the right thing to do. You, on the other hand, now know that you will waste hours of time and oceans of energy, with zero meaningful results if you do.

As an aside, I know there are those of you who are thinking that you got a client without all this ICA stuff. Yes you may have done, but what we're talking about here is a steady stream of inbound enquiries, not the odd client. 'Nuff said.

Consistency In Showing Up

What consistency looks like depends upon which marketing methods that you need to use in order to be where your ICA is.

Consistency Can Be...

- Consistency can be sharing useful content and insights on social media.
- Consistency can be regular attendance at a networking meeting (attend only those that your ICA also attends)
- Consistency can be regularly inviting your ICA to book a call with you and then making that call enlightening for them.

Consistency Is...

- Consistency is making sure that your message is focused

and targeted and that it doesn't wander off into different subjects or coaching specialities.

- Consistency is giving a clear call to action at the end each opportunity you get to communicate with your ICA, be that verbally, or in writing.
- Consistency is simply showing, regularly, with your message, even when you don't want to.

The rinse and repeat part is that once you have your ICA defined, and your message honed, then your job is to deliver it, regularly and reliably. Forever. That's it. There's no trick to this, you simply have to show up, where your ICA is, with your message.

Saying The Same Thing Over And Over

I am occasionally told by coaches that they feel awkward saying the same thing, over and over again. Let me assure you that this isn't a problem. On social media, you will be in front of different people each time you post. Social media posts have such a short life span that your ICA won't see every single thing you post. They'll see some of it, and they'll begin to see a consistent message.

There's a marketing acronym that I mentioned in an earlier chapter that is useful to understand. It's AIDA.

A – awareness
At this point, your ICA doesn't know you exist. They are completely and utterly unaware of you.

I – Interest
Once you move onto the radar of your ICA, which you do by

being consistent, you move into their consciousness and you generate interest. It's mild interest at this point.

D – Desire

When you've been on your ICA's radar for a while, they will start to become curious about what you do. They move from being interested to wanting to know more about your work and how you can help them. They start to desire to know more.

A – Action

The last step in this 4-step process is for your ICA to take some action in relation to you and what you do. This is where they respond positively to your call to action, and actually take action.

When you first start to deliver your message, providing you deliver it where your ICA hangs out, you will move people from never having heard of you, to a position where you exist at the periphery of their consciousness. This is them becoming aware of you (the A of the acronym) As you continue to deliver your message, your existence moves from the outer reaches of someone's mind, to a more aware area. At this point, assuming you're saying something that they are actually interested in, you've started to move them from A towards I in that acronym. The more you show up, with this interesting message, the more interested they will become.

Once they are conscious that they know what you're saying, and they are actively interested, continuing to see your reliable, clear and relevant message will move them to the D for desire; they will want to know more about what you do. They may seek you out online to have a look at how you show up in the world and to see if they're correct in their understanding that you are offering what they want.

Finally, your message will be so strong in their heads that they move to the final A and take some action. That action might be booking a call, sending you an email, or sending you a private message. This isn't the sale, but it's the next best thing. It's a warm enquiry.

Your job as a coach is to take that warm enquiry, have a conversation and turn it into a sale. You can absolutely do that, because you're a fabulous coach. I know that you can do this, because of the literally thousands of coaches with whom I have spoken, who tell me that once they actually sit down for a coaching conversation with someone, they usually end up with a client.

Be Consistent

I've said it before, but I'm going to say it again: Be consistent.

Be consistent with your message, with your presence and with your frequency of delivering your message.

Showing up briefly – and shouting loudly across various platforms, on or offline – doesn't' work. We've all seen those coaches who light up a platform with memes and claims of glory. The attend networking events and seem to be everywhere. They burn brightly, but briefly, before they disappear in a puff of smoke and you never hear from them again.

Being consistent wins. Showing up, regularly and frequently, even when you don't want to, wins. Don't expect to define your ICA, sort your message and then post half a dozen times and get clients. That's not how it works.

The process we teach is one that equips you to be in it for the long haul. You need to be where your client is, with the message designed for them and stay there. Day in and day out. This consistency does something subliminal. It marks you as reliable.

People come to see you as someone who does what they say they're going to do, even though you haven't explicitly said that what you're going to do is simply **be** there. What might feel to you like a chore – thinking of something to say/write every day – looks like reliability to your potential client. They learn to trust you, because you show up, with a consistent message and you do it regularly and frequently.

Quality Is Better Than Quantity

One of our mentees said recently that the reason they post so infrequently on social media is that quality is better than quantity. Honestly that's just not true!

If you post once every three weeks, your message will not get seen. It will disappear in the feeds of those you wish to attract. You need to show up every day. Quantity is just as important as quality!

Repurpose Your Content

One of the most marvellous things about the marketing message that you've created is that you can use it anywhere. Specifically, you can use it anywhere your ICA is; there's no point using it somewhere else, because then your ICA won't hear you, will they?

Repurposing content is something that people get really mixed up about and this chapter of this book is going to dispel myths and make repurposing content seem the natural thing to do – which by the way, it is, because it will save you hours of time and effort. Repurposing content is when you take something you have already created (like your full marketing message) and use it to create different forms of content.

Definition Of Social Media Marketing Terms

Just for clarity, I thought I'd define some terms you may come across when talking about social media marketing.

'Organic reach' means the number of people that see the post (that's the 'reach' part) without spending money on paid advertising (that's the 'organic' bit).

'Short form' posts are around 1000 words or fewer. Short

form posts are used to connect and engage your ICA. Short form posts can be skimmed and scanned.

A 'long form post' is generally considered to be a post of 1200-2000 words. Long form posts are used to educate and inform your ICA and generally require more conscious engagement and critical thinking.

What Is Content?

Content is anything you create in order to get your message out into the world. Content can be written, spoken, recorded, live... It is anything you say to your client to help them understand what you do. It is created from any part of your marketing toolkit that you could share. By the time you've reached this chapter of the book, you should have crafted your marketing toolkit. That's content. It's content that you can stand up and deliver as a talk, you can deliver it as a conversation, or you can break it down into smaller pieces and deliver it as engaging content in different forms.

Let me give you some examples of content forms:

- YouTube videos
- Long and short form Facebook posts
- Long and short form LinkedIn posts
- Articles and blogs (same thing, just named differently depending upon where you put them)
- Instagram images/posts
- Podcasts
- Alexa Flash Briefings (mini daily podcasts)
- LinkedIn or Facebook 'lives' (livestreamed videos)

- Memes (images with words on)
- Tweets

Each of those can be extrapolated from your marketing toolkit. For example, you can take tiny pieces of your marketing message and turn those pieces into questions.

Let me give you some examples:

New manager

- Do you find you're losing sleep worrying about your new team?
- Do your team members need to be your friends?

Mumpreneur

- Do you know how many/much of your product/service you have to sell in order to reach your financial goals?
- Do you actually have a financial goal?

Retiree

- How many years of retirement do you intend to have?
- How many of those will you enjoy?

How To Use Those Questions As Content

Those questions can be a post in themselves, or they can be the impetus for you to write a longer post.

You could create videos in which you pose any of those questions, and then offer some insight into how your ICA might be feeling about them. Remember, we have our marketing heads on here, not our coaching heads, so you are free to offer up potential solutions.

You could take one of those questions and extrapolate the answer into an article, or a podcast.

Don't Reinvent The Wheel

When you're repurposing content, you don't need to reinvent the wheel. The main reason you don't is that you already *have* the wheel, your marketing toolkit, which comes from your marketing message.

The secret about repurposing content is that you take your message down to its component parts. Look at it carefully. Where you've asked questions, use them as article (or blog) titles and answer them; you've already answered them in your message, just turn that message into an article, or podcast or video etc.

Saying The Same Thing, Over And Over

It's easy to get hung up on the fact that you're repeating yourself in some of your social media content. It's a very common worry. Let me put your mind at rest. The lifespan of a social media post is small and not everyone will even see every post. If you look at my LinkedIn profile and examine the articles I've written, and the posts I've shared, you'll see that I stick to a theme with my content.

That theme is my marketing message, the one I created for Stella Hewitson. I don't deviate from that message, because it has served me very well in terms of generating awareness and attracting interest from those who fit my ideal client profile. Those are of course, the people who will benefit most from working with me.

The Lifespan Of Social Media Posts

Some statistics about the lifespan of any individual social media post that are current at the time of writing (2019). For the record, I got these stats from places like Hootsuite and Buffer; reputable companies who have scheduling software. That means their data is fresh and likely to be sound.

Facebook – 5 to 6 hours

Organic reach on Facebook is limited, remember, Facebook generates income from paid advertising and so they limit organic reach. Video has the most reach, followed by photos, then links and then text. Livestreaming video has the highest organic reach and the longest lifespan.

LinkedIn – 48 hours

Like Instagram, LinkedIn posts have a lifespan of around 48 hours. However, what you will notice with LinkedIn is that you occasionally get someone commenting or liking an old post, which will give it a new lease of life.

Instagram – Up to 48 hours. Stories 24 hours

Posts in the Instagram feed will have engagement for days if content is good and appropriate hashtags are used. Stories last 24 hours and can also be saved in profile with titles.

Pinterest – Up to 3 months

Pins can have engagement after a year if the content is engaging and the post is optimised for key words. Purchase intention is higher than other social channels.

Twitter – 15 to 20 minutes

The short lifespan of a tweet allows you to tweet exactly the same thing at different times and days and reach new audiences. You can also tweet many times a day. Photos and videos do best.

A Word Of Caution

Before you read the above and decide that Pinterest seems to be the best bang for your buck, remember this; this whole social media marketing isn't about you and where you think the least work lies, it's about your ICA and where they are. If they're not on Pinterest, then you're wasting your time and energy being there.

Break Down Your Message

A very good exercise to do is to break down your message into its component parts. You started with 10 separate sections, go back to those. Each of them has at least 10 separate things you can use as impetus for content.

Let me give you examples of prompts I can create from my marketing message:

- are you finding engaging clients tougher than you thought?
- are your strategy sessions bringing you paying clients?
- are you floundering with your marketing?
- where is your next coaching client coming from?
- it's not your fault that you can't find clients, you haven't been taught how
- would you like a pragmatic process for gaining paying clients?

Can you see what I've done? I've gone through my marketing message and taken it to bits. Those bits are gold; they are the individual tools that are contained within that toolkit. I can write whole articles about each of those prompts. I could make a video about each of them.

The time you spend breaking your marketing message (your tool box) down to its component parts, (your individual tools) is time that's incredibly well spent.

Analyse the Data

Once you have your ICA and marketing toolkit sorted, and you know where you need to be, the next step is data analysis.

Examples of the kind of data you need to record is this;

- Which of your posts or articles got the biggest engagement? Why?
- How did each initial coaching conversation go?
- What was the outcome?
- What did the potential client say?
- How did you leave the conversation? (Who has the ball?)

Having this data to hand is helpful. Our mentees share it with their mentors and go over it together. Interesting things emerge from data analysis.

Giving Away Too Much

One of our mentees was brilliant at generating the inbound enquiries, but then fell at the next hurdle. He wasn't turning any of them into paying clients and couldn't understand why.

When he and his mentor went over the data together, they were able to see that this mentee was moving into the realms of mentoring in the initial coaching conversation. What I mean by this is that he was telling the potential client what they needed to do to solve their problem. This meant that they could go away and implement his advice. They didn't need him to help them do this.

I can hear you gasping and thinking that what he was doing was the complete antithesis of what we do as coaches. However, this coach was **utterly** focused on providing value in his initial coaching conversation and he really wanted to help. The problem that he had identified was one that had a number of solutions to it, and of course, working out which solution was best should have been the work of the client in their coaching journey together. However, in his effort to give tremendous value, the coach simply gave the potential clients a solution, and they all went away and implemented it.

Interestingly, even though the coach had annotated all of this, until he had an outside perspective – that of his mentor – he hadn't spotted what he was doing. Once he did, his game changed.

Tumbleweeds

If you find that you're posting and not getting much by way of engagement, then look hard at what you're posting. What language are you using? Are you using client-speak or have you slipped into coach-speak? I promise you, it's easy to slip into coach-speak.

Read your post from the point of view of the client. Is it interesting? Challenging? Controversial? Does it spark their imagination? Or is it bland? Bland doesn't get interaction, the others do.

Go back to your marketing message and pick out little bits of it that are close to the heart of your ICA. For example, I might mention that a coaching qualification doesn't equal paying clients, no matter how much the coach might want it to. I could also talk about 'hopeful' marketing. Coaches who are practicing it will prick up their ears. I could also talk about the longing my ICA has to coach for a living, and how much joy that would bring to their lives. Can you see how I'm breaking down my marketing message?

A Caveat

It may be that the problem you support your client to solve is one that they wouldn't want to publicly confess to having. For example, Alisa Barcan (former mentee and now mentor) works with people who simply can't manage their money. This isn't something that people want to admit to on LinkedIn. In particular, many of Alisa's clients are those who manage other peoples' money and have feelings of shame associated with the fact that they can't manage their own money, so definitely wouldn't admit to this in public.

However, although many of her social media posts don't get much in the way of engagement, her inbox is full of people who want her help.

Liz O'Neill is the same. She is also a former mentee and now a mentor. Her ICA is someone who manages teams of technology workers. They're 'nerds' as Liz calls them (she's allowed to, she's one herself!). Liz knows that her ICA is highly unlikely to engage on social media, but that hasn't stopped her from building a coaching business from those who hop into her inbox and say *hey Liz, you're talking about me*.

Acting Upon The Analysis

When you've analysed the data, you will end up with a list of posts that engage, and a list of those that don't. You'll have the detail of conversations that have resulted in paying clients, and those that haven't.

Look and learn from that list. Don't continue to post along the lines of topics that haven't got much engagement. I realise this seems like stating the obvious, but it's not. You'd be surprised how many coaches continue to simply churn out bland posts, despite the evidence.

Alisa Barcan – Revisited

Alisa started working with The Coaching Revolution in April 2018. I interviewed her in September 2018 and that interview can be read in chapter 6. I re-interviewed Alisa in February 2019, as there had been some exciting things happening in her business.

What follows is Alisa in her own words, from an interview we had together.

Tell Me About Where You Are Now?

Alisa said:

It is a very special day for me because today is the very first day that I'm working full-time in my business, because I've just quit my corporate job! I feel great! I've made sure that I have things planned for today, to make sure I don't treat it as a day off. Today is busy.

Tell Me About Your Career To Date

I'm a chartered accountant. I am known for my sound commercial acumen and so my most recent job was I that of commercial analyst for a fairly big company. It was still working with numbers and spreadsheets, but not in the way an accountant usually works.

What my role entailed was looking at the company revenue and costs, for six global regions, and analysing what was happening. I was working out what was going well and what was not for that company, and putting strategies in place to help the sales people in the field with whatever it was that they needed to get the job done.

I worked as part of the sales department, which meant a high-pressure and fairly stressed environment. I had to prepare financial reports that could be easily understood by non-financial employees. These reports had to be completed in a timely manner, because the information needed to be provided at a point where it was still useful. My job was to help sales people understand where their efforts were time well spent, and where it was time wasting. At the same time, we would look at costs and see whether they were being efficient at using the money that we were allocating for the type of activities they needed to do in order to get the sale done.

Is Commercial Acumen The Same As Business Development Skills?

No, they're different. Let me explain. Having commercial acumen means, for example, that from a company's point of view, you know what the demand is for the services or the products that that company offers. It means being aware of competitors in the market, and to be able to analyse your competitors' actions.

If, for example, you've got a competitor who's new in the market, why is that? What's happening on a local level that means that you've got a new competitor now? Are you performing poorly? Is there a niche market that has appeared of which you weren't aware? Do they have some competitive advantage over you?

There are many things to consider, but business acumen isn't the same as business development. It really helps to have a little bit of commercial acumen to then apply to your business development skills, but they are separate things.

Why Is Now The Right Time To Leave Your Job?

I'm very intentional with my time. I like to plan; I'm a planner. Therefore everything that was important made it to my calendar. I made full use of my calendar to really have a look and see where the best times and the best opportunities are for me to leverage.

An example is that I would take my full lunch break, and in that hour I would coach someone. I had a few clients that were my lunchtime clients, but I didn't do it every day because I don't really like eating 'al desko' all the time. Every few days I would have a client at lunchtime.

When I came home in the evening, I would allow time to eat and spend some time with my partner, but I would schedule that into my diary too. Everything that was important made it to my calendar. A few examples are; spending time with my partner, speaking to the parents and catching up with them and with friends. In short, everything I needed to fit into my day, went in my calendar.

The reason that I was so careful with my time is that I was trying to eliminate decision fatigue. The more I had to wonder about what I needed to do next, what the most important thing to do was. If I don't do this kind of scheduling, I find that before you realise it, half an hour is gone in choosing what to do next. I was very time poor and so it was really important for me to sit down on a Sunday and have a really good look at my calendar and see how I can leverage the time I had available. It does take discipline and a lot of work – extra work – but I found that it's really worth it because I knew exactly what I needed to do, and I just did it.

Building a business isn't just about seeing clients. Building a business is also making sure that you go and see people and you let them know what you do, and that you create content for your social media platform(s) or for your website if you have one. All of that has to happen around you coaching clients. So yes, it was a huge 'time jigsaw puzzle' but that's how I did it.

It's also important to mention that I really saw my partner as a true partner. I think Sheryl Sandberg mentions this in her book, *Lean In*. She talks about really seeing your partner as a true partner and splitting responsibilities with them. In my case my partner is wonderful, and he would support me with the things that I had to do at home. He'd basically do the housework for me if he knew that I had a client, or a networking event for example. I made use of all the resources I had and that's how I managed to fit everything in.

I didn't leave things to chance. I know I'm responsible for the things that I want to create, and if I am responsible then I'm going to take responsibility. Part of that responsibility is to know what it is that I needed to do.

If you have to keep wondering what to do, then, of course, you're not going to do anything at all. However, when you take some time to think about, what your priorities are, and what you need to do (and in what order) to actually achieve them, then you can start thinking in a different way. What that means is that you actually do things rather than worrying about not knowing what to do. We all know this, but we don't often apply it, do we?

I feel obliged to say that I don't advocate to go and do this if it really goes against who you are and doesn't resonate with what you believe in. However, you can still incorporate some of this planning and not have your calendar completely full. Maybe you can plan for two days a week to focus on something else, to be creative and do whatever you fancy and see what works for you.

For me, it works to have everything planned in advance because as I said, I don't like decision fatigue. I didn't have a lot of time and, because I am naturally such a planner, if I hadn't already organised what I was going to do and why, then before I start any an activity, it would take me about half an hour just to plan what I needed to do.

To put this into context, let me give you an example. When I come back from work and have a client from 6:30pm for an hour, and then write notes for another half an hour, that takes me to 8pm. If at that point I had to start thinking 'now what do I need to do' it would be 9pm before I'd decided what was most important. Remember, I also needed to fit in normal things like showering and make sure that I got to bed at a reasonable time.

For time-poor people, my advice would be for them to use whatever it is that works for them, but to be willing to try new things. It's really important for us to not think about planning as being a constraint, but something that's going to take us to where we want to go.

How Do You See Your Relationship With The Coaching Revolution Evolving?

I find that we coaches have this idea that once we get clients, then all our problems will go away. That's just not true. What happens is that you just get a different type of problem. For perhaps some of your clients might be more difficult, or they struggle with the concept of coaching. Perhaps the work that you do with them reminds you of something which is very emotional for you. What I'm saying is that you get different types of problem.

I have to say that having different problems shows growth and change, but it's so important to have people around you that you can discuss these things with. You need to be surrounded by people who will understand what it is that you're going through *because they have been through it before.*

I'm now a Coaching Revolution mentor. What that means is that not only do I get to support my own mentees, I can speak to other people who are mentors themselves to talk about issues I might be having. I can also talk with mentees who have reached success themselves and to be able to have intelligent conversations about the practice of coaching is very valuable. It's something that's really important. It fulfils a similar function to coaching supervision, and that's something that's required as a continuing professional development CPD for a coach.

Once again, it's all about community. For me, that's really important. Just to have someone there that you know you can trust to give you advice from experience, not from get knowledge from just reading stuff in a book. I *could* go and read it myself, but I want to know from a real person who's done it. I want to ask 'how did you deal with this situation?' and 'what kind of ideas do you have?' It's very useful because if you as a coach are trying to, for example, move into group coaching or creating programmes, you can just ask and get some feedback. I am very confident that the feedback I get is really honest. I find it so much more helpful than trying to glean knowledge by asking questions in a Facebook group for example.

What I notice in particular, is that a lot of the coaches in our community are the ideal clients of some of the others. What that means is that they can give feedback from the point of view of the kind of client you want to attract. It means that if you ask them what they think, you can be confident that you will be asking someone who has a lot in common with the person who would buy from you. That makes the feedback very valuable. It's so much better than just asking some random people what they think. The more often we can have conversations with people who we know fit our ideal client profile, the better and clearer our marketing messages will be for example.

What Next For Alisa Barcan, Financial Coach?

I'm looking forward to working on and in my business. My next task is to think about my website. The Coaching Revolution mentors were very clear with me at the beginning that it would be a mistake to get bogged down in worrying about what colours my branding needed to be, or how my website should look, so I don't have a website yet. Just think, I've managed to create a full-time income from coaching, without a website!

It's absolutely true that a coach can create a brand, inspire trust and grow their business with nothing more than a good social media presence. I'm living proof of it.

Cool Tools

As part of our journey together, I thought I'd share some useful real-life stuff with you. I use lots of online tools to automate and simplify my business. In this short chapter, I'll share with you the ones I use. Remember, I'm writing this in 2019, and things move quickly, so depending upon when you're reading this, you might want to check if what I've said is still true.

Online Scheduler

I use AcuityScheduler.com. I like it because I find it easy to use, easy to synchronise with my online diary and easy to add questions to the booking form.

Synchronising a scheduler with an online diary means that you can never double book yourself. I get to select when I'm available for appointments and then Acuity checks my diary and displays availability based on the gaps it finds in my available hours. I can even factor in the maximum number of calls that can be booked in a day and add some padding to the end of each call so that they don't end up back-to-back in my diary.

I pay for Acuity, somewhere in the region of £15 a month. I think it's worth it because I no longer have that 'backwards and forwards with alternative dates' nonsense. It's also almost always my CTA, so I use it all the time.

Others you can use are calendly.com and meetfox.com

With all 3 of these, you can actually use it to take payment for coaching sessions at the time of booking, which means you ever have to chase an invoice again.

Client Relationship Manager (CRM)

We use HubSpot. We use it for everything up to and including welcoming new mentees on board.

The 'everything' of which I speak goes like this:

- we enter an enquiry into HubSpot, including details like the obvious stuff; emails, phone number etc, but also where they heard about us, and where they are geographically.
- we send tracked emails out from HubSpot. We can see when they are opened, and whether or not various links have been clicked.
- we have a number of template emails that we use so that we have good continuity. What I mean by that is that we know exactly what people have had, without having to trawl through a sent box.
- we can change the status of the entries to reflect where they are in our process. For example they can be new, in progress or joined.

We use the free version of HubSpot and it has served us

well. There are paid versions that do other whizzy things, but we've never needed them.

Podcast Software

Our podcast, **Coffee With The Coaching Revolutionaries**, is managed on Anchor.fm.

This is a free platform, that will distribute your podcast to 11 other platforms without you having to do a thing. Our podcast is on Spotify, Stitcher, Apple podcasts, Google podcasts and several others. I didn't actually know half of these platforms existed!

The way Anchor.fm works is that you upload a recording of your most recent episode, and then Anchor does the rest.

Anchor also has an app that you can use to actually record your podcast on your phone. It's incredibly easy.

Image Creation

For images of all shapes and sizes, we use Canva.com. We pay for the business version, but the free version is plenty to start with.

You can create almost any image you want, for anything you need it for. We use their templates for things like Facebook posts, and their 'custom size' feature for things like our blog-post images.

A word of caution here, it's very easy to spend a happy day playing on Canva. Remember that your goal is paying clients, not beautiful images!

Book Writing

I know I could have used Word to write this book, but instead, I used Dabblewriter.com. I pay about £8 a month for it.

I like the way that it organises the chapters etc. Basically, it's far more logical than I am, and not only that, it keeps a track of words; the final goal, the total written so far, how many have been written today, in this chapter etc. I find this really helpful.

Transcripts and Captions

Rev.com is where we go to get transcripts of recordings we've made or captions for videos. They charge $1 a minute and their turnaround is about 24 hours. There is not monthly fee.

The case study chapters are taken from transcripts of podcast episodes in which I interviewed the mentees. Obviously, they're not straight transcripts because we don't speak in the same way that we write, so there was lots of editing to do.

Video Editing

We use Kapwing.com to edit videos. We take the .srt files (caption files) that we buy from rev.com and add them to the video. We can also add logos, front and back cards etc.

Kapwing does lots of things that we don't use. If video is your thing, the $20pm fee is probably worth it.

We're also investigating the editing facilities that YouTube is now offering. They're always worth checking, because they change on a regular basis.

Communication

The Coaching Revolution mentors and support staff use Slack.com to communicate. We can share files as well as text.

Slack allows you to group people, so we have a mentor group, an ICF course group and a general group.

We use the free version and it's served us well.

Organisation

We use Trello.com to keep track of mentees progress. Each mentor updates the mentee's board after the session.

We don't, of course, share personal stuff, we share progress, and tasks assigned, plus anything that would be handy for someone to know if they had to take over the next session unexpectedly.

I also use Trello to keep track of my work, and I share this board with my VA, so that we're singing from the same hymn sheet without having to constantly update each other on Slack.

Email Automation

We use ActiveCampaign.com to organise and schedule our email list and emails. We chose to move from MailChimp as our list got bigger, partly because my VA was much more familiar with it than she was with MailChimp. We pay for ActiveCampaign.com, because of the size of our email list.

I can state for the record, that MailChimp is a great place to start with automating your emails. One of the reasons that you simply must use something like MailChimp or ActiveCampaign, is because if you start using email marketing, you have to give people a simple way to unsubscribe, and email marketing software puts an unsubscribe button in the footer of each email.

There are myriad rules around GDPR that could impact what you do with your mailing list. They are outside the scope of this book. If you want to know more about GDPR and how it affects you, can I recommend Suzanne Dibble's book *GDPR for Dummies*?

Au Revoir

So, we've reached the end of this part of our journey together. You now know everything you need in order to market your coaching business. I'm not going to say goodbye, because that feels too final. Let's just say au revoir, because I'm sure our paths will cross again.

A good place to start our paths crossing is **Coaching Republic.** Might I reiterate that invitation to join Coaching Republic? It's our free Facebook community for coaches just like you. Hop over to Facebook and search for us? We're all there, waiting to say hello, so come on over!

Help With Implementation?

Knowing how to build a coaching business, and actually building one are two different things. The thing I can't offer you in this book is 1:1 support and the accountability that goes with that.

I'm sure you've reached the conclusion that we at The Coaching Revolution know what we're doing. If you'd like to have a chat with me about working 1:1 with your own mentor, why not hop over to our website and click on any of the buttons that says **book a call**? I'd be delighted to talk to you, and we can discuss how The Coaching Revolution might be able to help you. A conversation with me costs nothing, and it has been the starting point for many successful coaching businesses.

Au revoir and good luck!

with love
Sarah x

Acknowledgements

There are several people without whom I simply wouldn't have finished this book.

I'd like to thank Sarah Gilligan, my Australian champion for reading and re-reading the book. Lots of the clarification you've read comes from Sarah's input. Sarah is a Coaching Revolution mentee.

I'd like to thank Paul Snell for being Paul Snell. One of The Coaching Revolution founders, endlessly supportive, massively patient and tremendously encouraging.

Thanks to my mum (Nancy Kearney) and Helen Clare for proof-reading and editing.

In addition, I'd like to thank Kathryn MacNeill for listening to me complain that it was too hard, and Martin Robson for helping me keep track of the word count. I'm so grateful to have both of you in my life.

I'd like to thank Verity and Honor, my daughters for always simply assuming that I can and will do anything I set my mind to. When I see the utter confidence in me in the faces of my grown-up children, I can't fail, can I?

Finally, I'd like to thank The Coaching Revolutionaries, without whom none of this would have happened. In particular, I'd like to thank those who have allowed me to interview them, some of those interviews you have read in the preceding chapters. Alisa, Liz, Jenny, Jeff, Sarah – thank you.

Printed in Great Britain
by Amazon

18956209R10133